Orphan care is warfare. Whether you set out to adopt children, or care for orphans in a variety of other God-reflecting ways, you will face obstacles and opposition. But it's worth it. The Parkison's story of adoption highlights the real trials and the deep joys of sacrificial love. It also magnifies the grace of God needed for such an endeavor, and the grace that God has shown us, as His adopted children. Read and be edified!

—TONY MERIDA
Pastor for Preaching and Vision, Imago Dei Church, Raleigh, NC
Co-Author of *Orphanology*

Our hearts must be open to the Lord, His mission, and what He might have us do. In *He Knows Her Name*, Kelly Parkison reminds us to "never say never," and to trust the Lord's work in our hearts and minds.

—ED STETZER
LifeWay Research

Kelly McCorkle Parkison's heart for adoption and helping orphans is not only admirable, it's contagious! As an adoptive father myself, I can relate to the emotional roller coaster the adoption process can be. I was deeply moved by Kelly's journey of faith and encouraged by her resolve to triumph over every obstacle. *He Knows Her Name* is a transparent and honest look into the heart of a sold-out believer seeking to be the hands and feet of Jesus to the least of

—KYLE SHERMAN
ermanMusic.Com

May I commend the precious story of perseverance, compassion, and honesty in the context of this adoption story. Having known

Scott and Kelly for years, I commend to you their testimony, this story, and their walk in the Lord. It will bless you as it did me.

—Dr. Frank Page
President and CEO of the Executive Committee
of the Southern Baptist Convention

Kelly Parkison tells a compelling and courageous story . . . her own. While the will of God takes some people around the world, it was during a nationally televised trip around the world that this remarkable lady found the will of God.

During Kelly's journey God allowed her to see a sea of people without Him and without hope. It broke her heart. And then the Lord reshaped that heart into the heart of a missionary. And that heart would become the heart of a mom . . . an adoptive mom.

The personal and transparent way it is written makes this the best book I've ever read on adoption. The journey that Kelly and her Pastor-Husband Scott take leads them to adopt a beautiful little girl. HE KNOWS HER NAME . . . and soon, you will also.

—Dr. Randy C. Davis
President and Executive Director
Executive Board of the Tennessee Baptist Convention

As an adoptive mom myself, I was completely drawn in from the first sentence. This beautiful story is an amazing one of God's perfect timing and complete sovereignty when His children listen to His call. Kelly's story is so moving, and one told so anyone choosing to adopt could certainly follow the process. Many times as I read, I felt myself being transported back to the six adoption trips we have made. Each one with its own harsh realities and great blessings. Thank you Kelly for sharing your heart, your testimony, your family, and your adoption journey. We are more blessed because of your willingness to write and allow us to read. Hoping many orphans find their forever family because someone hears God's call on them as well.

—Sharon M. Ankerich
Everythingbeautifulshay.blogspot.com
and Growingwholehearts.blogspot.com

Kelly is a woman of faith. She travels daily the path that God has shown her. She is a blessing in my life and this book will be a blessing to you.

—Rep. Rita Allison
South Carolina House of Representatives

Gracing the stage of the Miss America Pageant and competing on *The Amazing Race* both pale in comparison to the adventure that my friend Kelly Parkison has been on in recent years. In *He Knows Her Name*, this pastor's wife and mother of five takes us along with her to the land of India as well as the depth of her soul to remind us that we don't have to be on a mission trip or adopt a child to be used by God. We just need to be available and obedient. With a voice that's refreshingly honest and beautifully transparent, Kelly pulls back the curtain of the journey that awaits those who are obedient to love one more.

—Jennifer Slenk
Revive Our Hearts Ministry Area Ambassador

Anyone who has answered a call to serve God and walk by faith and not by sight will find *He Knows Her Name* inspiring and edifying. While *He Knows Her Name* is the beautiful story of Kelly meeting the little girl her family will adopt, it also is the transcendent story of Kelly meeting the God who knows and calls each of us by name.

—Erika Harold
Miss America 2003

HE KNOWS HER NAME

an amazing pursuit to adopt from India

Kelly McCorkle Parkison

AMBASSADOR INTERNATIONAL
GREENVILLE, SOUTH CAROLINA & BELFAST, NORTHERN IRELAND
www.ambassador-international.com

He Knows Her Name:

An Amazing Pursuit to Adopt From India

ISBN: 978-1-62020-505-1

eISBN: 978-1-62020-409-2

Cover Design and Page Layout by Hannah Nichols
eBook Conversion by Anna Riebe Raats

AMBASSADOR INTERNATIONAL
Emerald House
411 University Ridge, Suite B14
Greenville, SC 29601, USA
www.ambassador-international.com

AMBASSADOR BOOKS
The Mount
2 Woodstock Link
Belfast, BT6 8DD, Northern Ireland, UK
www.ambassadormedia.co.uk
The colophon is a trademark of Ambassador

Dedicated to the waiting orphans across the world, hoping to be the next child to have a real family.

Acknowledgments

To God be the glory for all He has provided.

To my husband who has been my spiritual mentor and who has laid the foundation of our family on solid rock. You are my most favorite! You are my beloved and you are my friend (Song of Solomon 5:16). I love you.

To my five children, who would wait patiently and let me say, "Just a minute" while I wrote our story for this past year. You are a great reward from the Lord and it is my privilege to be your Mom. I love watching you grow and I am excited to see what the Lord has planned for you. I love you very much!

To my extended family for unlimited support and encouragement not only during this writing, but during my entire life.

To our churches where we have served, Taylors First Baptist of South Carolina, Wakefield Baptist of North Carolina, and especially, our church home, Trinity Baptist of Manchester, Tennessee. God used so many of you to prepare our way and to serve and to assist along the journey and to encourage us as our story continues.

To all the friends and strangers literally across America, who accepted God's nudges to lift us in prayer and to donate their time, their talents, and their money; God knows each and every name.

To Lyla's doctors and nurses in India and her doctors in America; thank you for caring for her heart and health as if she were your own,

To Lyla's teachers and to Westwood Elementary; you were an integral part of her adjusting to her new world due to your acceptance of her and your watch care over her; she is learning more and more and progressing due to your patience and diligence.

To all the many, many people who assisted with fundraising events or made donations for us to use to solicit funds.

To the Indian Mommas, for the advice, encouragement, and camaraderie.

To our missionary friends, new and old, serving God in India and meeting our needs in so many ways; we pray for you daily.

To Dr. Hagin and North Greenville University for inspiration to do God's work; and to Hopegivers for caring about the needy people in the world and thus opening my eyes to be a part of such a worthy mission.

To our fellow churches who partner with us in Loft 218.

To Tim and Alison Lowry, and Ambassador International, who believed our story could make a difference in others.

To Brenda Covert for being such a wonderful editor and for making my book more readable; and to the staff of Ambassador International for your hard work and dedication.

To the readers; thank you for purchasing and sharing our story with us. Your purchase will support Loft 218 as we seek to do more for orphans, widows, and victims of sex trafficking in India and in America.

Contents

FOREWORD

KNOWING A BIT OF KELLY'S story, I was really honored when she asked me to write the foreword to her book. I figured that I probably wouldn't find out much more than what I already knew, but boy was I ever surprised!!! I literally could not put this book down. The story of Kelly's journey from being named Miss South Carolina in 2002 eventually leading her to be chosen as a participant in the CBS reality show, *The Amazing Race*. Kelly's goal was to win the one million dollar prize, but 11 countries later she knew beyond a shadow of a doubt that God had a much greater purpose in mind for her journey.

The one country that Kelly knew she never wanted to see or visit again was India, and yet this is the one country that her heart is now so very connected to. I do not want to give the story away, but I will tell you that I think this book should be made into a major motion picture film. This story is so compelling, because what God put in Kelly's heart about India was there to stay. She eventually returned to that nation on a mission's trip where she would fall in love with the orphans she met at one particular orphanage. This seed that was planted would bear fruit years later when Kelly and her husband, Scott, would return to India to adopt a child from the very country of which she said she would never return.

I can speak firsthand of Kelly as a person because I actually had her come to our Tennessee Mercy home in Nashville and speak to our residents and staff. I should have known after hearing Kelly speak that I would love her book, because I thought she was one of the greatest speakers that I had ever heard. There is no way that I can do this book justice by trying to explain the impact it had on my heart as I read every word of the manuscript. I totally related to Kelly's feelings about wanting to make sure that these children were loved and cared for. Let me explain . . .

Not too long after founding Mercy in 1983, God spoke to my heart to open our doors to young women facing unplanned pregnancy. Though I have never adopted a child, over the years I have seen multitudes of young women walk through the doors of Mercy who prayerfully made the choice for adoption. As a result of being involved in hundreds of adoptive placements and meeting the adoptive families, I so related to everything Kelly and Scott went through as she described how their story unfolded. I recognized the tension between the agony of waiting and the trusting of God's perfect timing. I recognized the provision of God and how it is His heart to take care of orphans and to place the solitary in families. I also recognized that God did for Kelly and Scott what I had seen Him do in so many other adoptive couples that I knew personally . . . He placed a supernatural love in their hearts so that they loved their adopted child from India just as much as they loved their own biological children.

One day I received a phone call from Kelly asking me to meet her for lunch. It was then that I learned about the desire and passion that God had placed on Kelly and Scott's hearts to start their own 501C3 charity. This organization would come to be known as *Loft 218,* and its purpose would be to not only support couples going through the process of international adoption, but also to serve orphans, widows, trafficking victims, and the oppressed of India. I knew immediately that God was speaking to me to step up and do for Kelly and Scott what others had done for me in 1983 when I first started Mercy. The first step was to legally establish the organization, and it was such a joy to be able to sow the first financial seed to make that possible.

Years later, this organization is now established and in full operation. You can learn more on their website www.loft218.com. If our hearts truly belong to God, then we should have a heart for those who have been orphaned or oppressed, for whatever reason. Maybe God will stir your heart to become part of the answer . . .

—Nancy Alcorn
Founder and President
www.mercymultiplied.com

Chapter 1

NEVER SAY NEVER

"THE WORLD IS WAITING FOR you. Good luck! Travel safe!" he said. Phil Keoghan, the host of the CBS reality show, *The Amazing Race*, raised his hand and his left eyebrow. "Go!"

I took off from that starting line in California, not knowing what lay ahead as I embarked on a journey around the world **and** my first trip outside the United States. My experiences on *The Amazing Race* exposed me to considerably more than I could have ever imagined. It stretched me as a person, as a competitor, and as a follower of Christ. Fortunately, I managed to remain in the race until the finale of the show, winning a few prizes and coming in third place overall. The competitor in me was disappointed that I did not win the million dollar prize, but as cliché as it sounds, I was a winner . . . I now know I won in the long run. What I saw and experienced on this amazing journey had changed me. I would never be the same.

During the filming of the show, Lima, Peru, turned out to be our first pit stop. We arrived early in the morning before the hustle and the bustle of the city had begun. After completing some required tasks for the race, we examined our surroundings and interacted with some of the local people. I remember glancing toward a hill-side and seeing colorful wooden boxes about the size of refrigerator boxes lined up in every direction. It took me a few minutes to realize my American view of suburbia and the middle class was being shat-tered. I soon recognized these multi-colored boxes were dwellings, and people with multiple children called them home.

In another leg of the race, we arrived at a South African orphan-age and delivered gifts to the precious children as part of our quest. This created yet another unforgettable memory. I was becoming in-creasingly aware of the tremendous needs in this world, and they were beyond anything I could have imagined. Coming face-to-face with such neediness began to penetrate my heart and mind. I felt guilty racing for the chance to win one million dollars, knowing these kids did not have what I had in South Carolina. Simple things like running water, electricity, a house, a car, or a family.

During the six weeks of filming the race, I was exposed to many other uncomfortable situations that led me to appreciate home and the cushy life I had been granted. I slept on a beach in Peru and at-tempted a shower with a water bag hanging from a tree branch. I observed the slum children of India bathing in sewage and I slept fit-fully sitting up in a filthy berth on a train. While in London, England, I begged for money in order to survive. We had been penalized on the race and were penniless. I empathized with the desperation of having no means by which to eat, to have shelter, or to change my circumstances for the better.

My participation on the show had promised an amazing experi-ence, and it truly changed my perceptions of the world. After return-ing from participating in this extraordinary reality show, I was only allowed to share a limited amount of information with my parents regarding my adventures during the show's filming. Because I had persevered to the end of the race, I had been fortunate to visit a total of eleven different countries. I told my parents, "I loved every place I visited during the race and would go back to every single country except for one: India." Once in India was enough for me. I expected never to return.

Why such dislike for India? It all started when we landed in the airport of Lucknow. I was already somewhat nervous about this new country. My overall concerns were validated as I visited the airport bathroom only to discover the famous "squatty potty." I was also shocked and disgusted by the lack of toilet paper! My anxieties mounted.

As we exited the airport, we were swamped with taxi drivers vying to carry our bags. They did not speak a word of English other than "hello," and some of them were trying to grab my bags from me as they encircled me. I had never been claustrophobic, but I felt my personal space quickly disappearing. I jumped in the closest taxi, perched on the edge of the seat with my backpack firmly in place, and felt relieved that my bag was no longer in danger of being snagged by strangers.

I had never been a germophobe, but I had this overwhelming fear that everything was nasty and dirty. It was the haze of smog outside, the pungent odors, and the appearance of uncleanliness everywhere. I remember thinking if I could limit what I touched, I would be safer. I tried to ball myself up as best as I could.. Not an easy task considering that, physically, I'm a pretty tall person, and I felt like a giant next to the Indian people. Every muscle in my body was cramping as I tensed up, working hard to be small. I was mentally on edge and literally on the edge of my seat in the taxi.

To make my insecurities worse, the taxi ride itself was quite a scary thrill ride as the driver darted hurriedly in and out of cars, rickshaws, pedestrians, and animals. To say the traffic and driving seemed crazy is an understatement. I was confused at the lack of traffic lights and stop signs. I thought there must be a law requiring every car to honk its horn every ten seconds because of all the constant horn honking! It was almost deafening at times.

I felt smothered as I looked out at the crowds of people everywhere. At home in the South, of course we had traffic and areas with overpopulation, but at home our traffic seemed more orderly, people and activity more spread out, and landscapes greener with more open space. Comparing this small town of Lucknow, India, to other places that I had lived, like New York and Washington, D.C., I determined our big cities in America are no more crowded or chaotic. There were crowds and crowds of people and commotion high and low. As I glanced around, I viewed shacks stacked atop each other and homes made from tarps in slum after slum. To add dismay to my first impression, small children were playing right beside this crazy dangerous road. Their safety concerned me, as did my own due to the noise, crowds, commotion, odors, and craziness. Everything seemed radically different from anything I had ever experienced. This culture was the complete opposite of my home sweet home in America.

We had made it through the traffic without incident, and I was somewhat relieved to exit the taxi, but still there were multitudes of people in every direction. Additionally, the camera crew from *The Amazing Race* hurriedly following us drew extra, unwanted-by-me

attention, while at times it appeared there were hordes of people passing us without even acknowledging the strange and somewhat frantic
American people running through the streets with a film crew.

India was the only location where I felt unsafe. Not unsafe as in
danger of attack, but unsafe due to my mental insecurities and being
physically uncomfortable with my surroundings. We finally reached
a stopping point in filming that episode of the race. I anticipated getting rest and relaxation and finally leaving India for a new country,
but . . . Nope! We were told that next we would board a train and head
to Jodhpur, another city in India.

The train was another discomforting experience. We were offered pillows that seemed dingy and horribly stained. We were
warned of theft on the trains. It was definitely not my most restful
night of sleep, nor a warm one; I refused to use any sheet or blanket
on the train except to huddle up and sit on. I didn't want to touch any
part of the seats or berths. The odors were strong. I decided some of
the odors and stains were tracked onto the train and berths by the
shoes of passengers carrying human and animal excrement found
along the streets. Of course, my berth seemed the nastiest and filthi-
est of all.

Thankfully, after exiting the train, I discovered Jodhpur to be less
jam-packed with people. Perhaps I was growing more accustomed to
the pandemonium and had determined to try and enjoy myself. I did
have a great time when I undertook the task of racing on a camel! I
actually climbed into the camel cart, and off we went! I loved it! I was
in my own cart away from the crowds, and I was in control of the
cart! I laughed as I yelled out to the camel, "Go faster! Go faster!" This
was one of the most thrilling times I experienced in the entire race.

After the camel-racing leg of the race ended, we were given some free time to relax and a chance to casually tour a more affluent area of Jodhpur. It was quite a change from everything else I had experienced thus far. It gave us a chance to take a peek at how others live in India. However, another incident happened in Jodhpur that added to my negative view of the country: my water bottle was stolen. I was grateful for my good fortune to visit this country, but as far as I was concerned, being there once was enough for me. I was determined to never, never travel to India again. However, as the saying goes, "Never say never."

After I returned from the race, watched it air on television, and settled back into the real world, I received a phone call from Dr. Linwood Hagin, the Dean of the Mass Communications Department at North Greenville University, my alma mater. He informed me he would be leading a media mission trip to India following the devastating tsunami that hit its coastline in December the year before.

According to the National Oceanic and Atmospheric Administration, "Tsunamis are giant waves caused by earthquakes or volcanic eruptions under the sea."[1] This particular tsunami destroyed many lives and left horrific damage in its wake. Dr. Hagin asked me to join the team since I had earned a bachelor's degree in Mass Communications from NGU in 2001. Ha! Was this a joke? I had resolved in my heart and verbalized as well that traveling to India was a one-time event for this girl. But Dr. Hagin's invitation continued to resound in my head and heart. God began to chisel away at my stubbornness and close-mindedness, and I realized Dr. Hagin wasn't the

---

1 National Oceanic and Atmospheric Administration, *What is a tsunami?* March 12, 2015, http://oceanicservice.noaa.gov/facts/tsunami.html.

one asking me to go to India. My Heavenly Father was urging me to go, and I couldn't shake it.

I'm not sure how long I fought God's call, but after a few weeks, I called Dr. Hagin back with my internally hesitant acceptance and said, "Yes, I will go if and *only* if I can raise the money in time."

This would be my first foreign mission trip. Unlike my last adventure to India, which had been completely paid for by CBS, I would need to raise every dime to finance the trip. Well, it didn't take long; God's provisions came pouring through, confirming to me He definitely desired my return to India. I was grateful for financial gifts from some of my church family members at Taylors First Baptist Church in Taylors, South Carolina, and additionally for numerous contributions from my close family and friends. Adding these donations to the additional money I earned accepting some public speaking opportunities, my trip was financed in no time. There was no turning back now! Also, Scott Parkison, the very handsome minister to single adults and college students whom I had been dating, encouraged me to take this trip and to confront my nervous anticipation about returning to India.

There were a few months to go before the NGU media mission trip. I had time to dwell on the mental images of the slums, the crowds, the traffic, the odors, and the little Indian children bathing in the sewage. I was preparing myself to be physically and emotionally miserable for the two-week trip. Our expedition to the coastline of India would take place only one year after the devastating Tsunami of 2004 and coincidentally, only a year after my *Amazing Race* experiences in India.

Our mission team would be partnering with an incredible organization called Hopegivers International. This organization serves orphans, lepers, dowry castaways, and AIDS victims; they provide educational assistance and plant churches in unchurched areas.[2] The purpose of all their activities is to glorify the kingdom of God. We would travel with Hopegivers to document all this ministry group had accomplished as well as document things the Indian government had done to help all of its tsunami victims.

This horrific tsunami had killed approximately 250,000 people in 14 countries and left thousands of orphans in its wake. In India alone, 18,045 people were confirmed dead, 5,640 were missing, and 647,599 people were displaced.[3] An additional purpose of this trip was to document what still needed to be done in hopes more Americans would be impassioned to help and to support these struggling tsunami victims, still in need a year after the tragedy.

For the media mission trip, we would be getting a ton of video footage, maybe conducting a few interviews, and perhaps recording documentation in journals. This was my introductory foreign mission trip, and I was excited to have my first media adventure on the other side of the camera. But, thanks to past experience, I knew what to expect regarding travel in India. I was thankful to globe-trot with Dr. Hagin and some great friends from church, which would surely make this trip a little more bearable! Nonetheless, little did I know and never could I have prepared myself for the stories of devastating loss, pain, and suffering and yet stories of human resilience I would

---

2 Hopegivers, *What we do*, accessed June 29, 2015, http://hopegivers.org.

3 Tsunami 2004, *Facts and Figures*, accessed October 1, 2015, http://www.tsunami2004.net/tsunami-2004-facts.

encounter. I was even more clueless as to the lasting impact it would have on my life.

We would connect with some others folks at the Atlanta airport on our travel day. So, early December 9th, we drove to Atlanta to join the rest of the team and the Hopegivers representatives. I met the quiet but friendly young lady I would be rooming with. Her name was Sarah. We all boarded the plane, and I was fully prepared for the long flight. After all, I was an experienced world traveler now!

When we landed in Mumbai, I was greeted with an old familiar smell: the mix of smog and rotting garbage. But this time around, it didn't bother me as much. We had arrived in the middle of the night, too tired to care! We taxied to our hotel and Sarah showed me, the world traveler (Ha!), how to operate the shower as she demonstrated how to flip a switch to heat the water for five minutes before turning it on. I discovered she had been to India before, but I still knew little about her with the exception of her first name. After my shower, I dressed in my pajamas and jumped in the bed. It was as hard as a rock! This hard, uncomfortable bed was unfamiliar to me. I was initially disappointed at the firm mattress, certain that I would wake up quite sore. But when I awoke, I felt rested and actually good. The extra firm mattresses were not so bad!

The next morning, Sarah and I had time to chat. She was so quiet that I probably talked her ears off. I noticed how she dressed so nice in a coordinated black outfit with cute wedge heels, while I had chosen sweat pants and a long sleeve tee shirt. I said to myself, *Maybe I got the wrong packing list, or is she crazy? Since she has been in India before, does she not remember all the filth that lies outside these doors?*

The team left the hotel, walking to begin our mission. I kept trying to convince myself to at least try to pretend to be comfortable and to ignore the odors and the noise all about me. First on our agenda was a tour of an orphanage. We walked a great distance down a back road to get there. As we arrived at the main building, I could see a welcome banner that the staff had hung near the facility that revealed an interesting fact about my roommate. The banner specifically listed the names of Dr. Hagin, the Hopegivers, and my roommate—Sarah *Zacharias*. It dawned on me that quiet, non-assuming Sarah was the daughter of Ravi Zacharias, a famous author, theologian, and Christian apologist, born in India but who now lives in America. Not only was she his daughter, but she was also a published author. She had been invited on this trip to write a book about the ministry of Hopegivers. Of course, Sarah is the kind of person filled with humility, who never would have promoted herself or her family name. We became quite close friends on the trip, and I admire her greatly.

As we entered the orphanage, I stared at the pile of little shoes sitting by the entrance. It is an Indian custom to take one's shoes off before entering a building. I worried as I took off my shoes that they might "go missing," just like my water bottle did during *The Amazing Race*. I noticed my shoes looked so gigantic next to the little children's shoes.

As we entered the building, precious little faces with huge smiles and eyes filled with curiosity were sitting quietly, organized in rows. We were greeted with

Holding a child orphaned by
the tsunami

these little smiling faces as they studied their strange-looking visitors. People must have been praying for me, or my heart could have melted right then and there. I was not nearly as anxious as I thought I was going to be.

An Indian orphan

The children loved having their pictures made, and they sang some songs for us. Another Indian custom is to exchange gifts and be extremely hospitable. From the richest family to the poorest family, Indian hosts insist on having visitors and serving them chai tea and biscuits. After performing their songs for us and serving us with refreshments, the children placed necklaces made of flowers around each of our necks—much like a Hawaiian lei. This was their gift to us.

We visited many other places in the surrounding areas of Mumbai: Kerala, Tenkasi, Chennai, and New Delhi. At each location, we documented stories from people victimized by the tsunami, or we saw orphanages now significantly over-populated because of the devastation left in its wake. We spent time in a leper colony, toured slums, and witnessed some of the government housing areas provided for families after the horrific destruction.

One housing area was more like a 10' x 10' shack made with metal sides and roof and a cement floor. As we entered their humble abode and interviewed some of the families living there, the heat was almost unbearable as it blazed down on the metal roof. Even though the conditions were extremely unfavorable, the residents were grateful to have a place to call home, as they had lost everything in the tsunami.

Each visit we made, each person we met, the things we observed, and the various stories we heard were all recorded and documented; unbeknownst to me, they were being etched in my heart forever.

THE FISHERMAN IN KERALA

We were on the coast of Kerala, interviewing a middle-aged gentleman with the help of a translator. We were literally standing on the beach; in the background of our video interview is the crashing sound of the waves rolling in. The man was a fisherman who had

Talking with the fisherman

been working on that very beach on the dreadful day, December 26, 2004. He said his day began like any other normal day. He was fishing from the beach, and suddenly the water was being pulled back out into the ocean. With tear-filled eyes he explained, "The water just sucked away." He described the numerous amounts of fish flopping all over the newly exposed beach. Many people, including him, went running out to grab as many fish as possible; fishing was how he made a living, and this could have been his largest and easiest catch ever. While he was gathering this gift of an abundance of fish, he looked up and saw walls of water, giant waves, moving toward him and the shore. He reported it was not just one wall, but several walls of water headed his way. Panic set in, and he and everyone else collecting fish dropped their armloads of fish and started running for shore. Then something he whispered struck me. "There was no warning. No one knew what was coming. No one knew anything was about to happen."

At home we have breaking news alerts ahead of time—Super Doppler warnings, sirens, television and radio alerts, or even news apps on our cell phones—to warn us of any danger headed our way. They did not have any of that technology. They had no warning of the disaster heading their way.

While he ran, his fears mounted for his family near the shore. How could he warn them? Watching the tears well up in his eyes now, I knew they did not get his wish for warning. He lost his wife, children, and grandchildren. It was pretty emotional for us all as we stood together and wept with him on the beach. I was curious about how he survived so close to the waves. He replied he had run as far as he could run before the water got to him, and he climbed up a coconut tree and held on as tight as he could.

After we left the fisherman, we continued to interview others. We viewed sites of property destruction and witnessed countless areas where homes had been completely wiped away. Many bare foundations were scattered near and far. We listened to and recorded more sad stories about the loss of children, the loss of spouses, or the loss of parents. But embedded in many of the stories were glimpses and glimmers of hope. They were rebuilding their lives. There were signs everywhere of the hope of new life. One sign of new life, I held in my arms: a precious baby girl born on that dreadful day, December 26th. Soon the baby would be one year old. Her parents named her *Tsunami*.

I learned a tsunami survival tip during numerous interviews, as people who were near the coastline stated they survived by holding on to a tree. Even later, as I researched online tsunami survival stories,

I read story after story of someone surviving because they held re-
lentlessly to a tree. Little did I know at the time, this analogy of holding on to a tree for hope and survival would help me through our
own adoption journey: *"Let us hold tightly without wavering to the hope
we affirm, for God can be trusted to keep his promise"* (Heb. 10:23, NLT).

At times, my hope in Christ and faith in God would be all that
would lead me through the trials of our adoption journey.

THE ORPHANAGE IN TENKASI

This orphanage was a larger facility run by a dynamic couple,
Sam and Elizabeth, who also operated a Christian school for their
community. Jesus radiated from their lives in their expressions of
laughter, joy, and love, which overflowed to the children around
them. Sam gave us the background history on the children. Each
child stood beside him as he told their personal story.

My heart ached listening to these reports of abandonment, dis-
ease, disabilities, and loneliness. Silently ashamed, I admitted to
myself I often took my family for granted. Why was I so blessed to
be born to the family I have? God had been gracious to me, but I
could acknowledge His bountiful grace to these children as well, as
He brought them to such a loving home. They now called Sam "Papa,"
and they were blessed with an earthly father. Each story Sam related
to us tore at my heart, but there were two that stuck with me.

One story was of a little three-year-old toddler found standing
at the entrance of their gate. They called out to her and asked her
name and what she needed; she had answered with one word that
translates "Simply." Sam explained she meant she had nothing but

simply herself. I was saddened for her having nothing, but even more touched by the divine appointment she had to end up at the orphanage gate. I couldn't imagine a little toddler wandering the streets of India—or any country—and miraculously ending up at the gate of a loving, Christian orphanage. God had taken care of her in a major way. The toddler was now twenty years old, and she stood beside Sam with a huge, beaming smile. Sam explained she would stay with them forever; due to some mental disabilities, she would never marry. He pulled her in close and, with his loud, joyous voice, exclaimed, "Elizabeth and I will be able to love on her longer!"

Next, a little blind girl with severe disabilities was brought to him, and as she reached Sam, she sat at his feet. Her story I did not expect. They found her out in a forest nearby; it was bizarre—she was being cared for by monkeys! They believe her parents abandoned her due to her disabilities, and monkeys found her and cared for her as if she were their baby. This story touched my core, and tears welled up in my eyes. Again, I was saddened she had been abandoned, yet happy she now lived in a clean, safe home.

The orphan wiping my tears

As I pondered all of this in my heart, tears began to flow freely, though quietly, down my face. I will never forget what happened next, and amazingly, it was caught on video by some of my team members. As I stood there silently weeping, the girl from the gate in the previous story came to me and reached up with her hands to wipe the tears from my face. The translator told me the girl was asking me not to be sad. I gave her the best smile I could manage, but she could not know how blown away I was that she, a girl who had been given little, would come to comfort and console me, a girl who had been given much. At that point, although trying to get control, I could not contain my tears. Even as I write this, I am still overwhelmed with emotion at her gesture that demonstrated the unselfish compassion of our Christ. I was reminded, *"He will wipe every tear from their eyes. There will be no more death or mourning or crying or pain, for the old order of things has passed away"* (Rev. 21:4, NIV).

THE GUPTA STORY

We visited the Gupta family home in Chennai. Daniel Gupta was born in India but moved to America and lived there most of his teen and early adult life. After becoming a successful businessman in California, God called him to return to his home to minister to those in his community of origin. His mother arranged a marriage to an incredible Indian woman, Vijay, and later they had two children. I was impressed that Daniel had chosen to leave America to become a missionary to his home country, but it was his testimony that would later affect my own life decisions.

He and Vijay had two biological children but felt led to adopt daughters due to the way the female class is often disrespected in India. The caste and dowry system basically devalues the lives of women and often leads to the abuse or death of old and young women or little girls. There are even many abortions that occur because the unborn baby is female. Daniel said that although no child deserved to be an orphan or on the streets, it was true young boys had a much higher survival rate, while young girls would be forced into the sex trade or traffic, made into house slaves, or even killed.

The Guptas did not adopt a few girls—they adopted *fifteen* girls and were raising them as their own children. This home was very different from the other homes we had visited. It was a literal house, much less like a dormitory or orphanage. It felt like a family—a very large family. I remember pledging to make a difference one day like this family.

Like Sam had done at the orphanage, Daniel told us the background of each of his daughters. Each one had a story touching and heartbreaking in its own way, but their joy in their new life was apparent. Vijay, being very musically talented, had been working with the girls. They put on a little concert for us that showcased the spectacular harmonies in their sweet little voices. We learned the girls were often invited to perform in various places around India.

After the concert and testimony time, the girls grouped together for our team so we could interact and take some photos. It was during this photo time something happened within my heart. Let me set the scene: at least forty people moved around in the room, generating lots of noise; the room was alive with the kids and the hustle and bustle of the mission team and the community folks who came for the concert. As the girls gathered for a group picture, I was frozen. While I could see all the movement in the room, I experienced only silence. My ears were deafened. During the silence, I felt and heard an urge loudly calling from my heart. God was speaking and calling to me. I knew one day I would adopt a little girl from India.

The noise and chaos reappeared, but I understood in that very moment the message I had received from God.

Later, I regarded it rather humorously. There I was, a single lady not even engaged to be married. I joked with God, "Well, okay, God, but You need to take care of the husband part first."

Ha! What a surprise to learn that God had been working on that part of His plan. While I was in India, my boyfriend of nearly a year, Scott, asked my parents for my hand in marriage! And I had no clue!

* * *

This trip reshaped me in so many ways. The country I once said I never wanted to visit again became a part of me. I had fallen in love with its people, its culture, its food, its clothes, and even its firm mattresses. I embraced the differences I had once found revolting and uncomfortable. How could I return to my wonderful, blessed life and leave all of these orphans behind?

When I arrived back in South Carolina, my family took me to breakfast to hear all about my trip. I could not even speak and began to cry. I was changed forever by what I saw and experienced. I couldn't even process it all. God had, as the expression goes, "rocked my world" with this trip. It took me days to be able to talk about it because I had left a piece of my heart in India. However, I kept to myself the message God audibly gave to me about adopting an Indian girl. I wasn't sure I was ready to share it, and I wasn't sure anyone was ready to hear it either.

Chapter 2

THE 411

ALTHOUGH I CHERISHED DISCUSSING MOST of the details of our mission trip with my family, I waited eagerly to disclose my personal spiritual call with my boyfriend, Scott. With a heart for missions, he had served on several international trips himself. I knew he would appreciate my story.

To give a little background, Scott and I were first introduced when he came to Taylors First Baptist as the singles pastor. I had won the title of Miss South Carolina 2002 and spent most of the following year traveling the state, speaking in other churches, so I was not often at my home church. The following year, I lived in Washington, D.C., and worked for Congressman Jim DeMint, who was campaigning to be elected to the United States Senate at the same time. My mother called me one Sunday to tell me she heard Scott speak that morning. Our conversation went like this:

Mom (hinting?):

> By the way, at church this morning that new singles pastor named Scott preached. He did a good job. Did you know he can also sing? AND did you know he can play the guitar too?

Me:

> Yes, I met him before and when I came home a few weeks ago, and I heard him speak and sing and play the guitar in my singles class.

Mom (obviously hinting now):

> I think he's handsome.

Me:

> I guess he's okay. But he doesn't date anyone that goes to our church because that's where he is serving in ministry.

Mom (determined!):

> Hmmm, that's dumb . . . well, you're not at the church. You're in Washington.

Me (nonchalantly):

> It will never happen, plus I'm dating someone.

My mom was not the only person trying to hint around at the idea of Scott and me dating. There were many people in the church who encouraged us to date.

Because Congressman DeMint was from Greenville, my hometown, his staff would come to the upstate occasionally to volunteer with the Senate campaign for the upcoming November election. Whenever I was in the area, I'd attend church and afterwards, fellowship with a group of the singles; on these occasions, I found Scott to be friendly, fun-loving, and yes, Mom, I admit . . . handsome.

Scott led a mission team from Taylors to Baltimore, Maryland. Since it was only an hour away from D.C., I joined them on the weekend. The more I was around this man, the more I found him very interesting. He truly desired to serve the Lord, and I found that most attractive.

After secretly being selected to begin preparations in the early fall as a contestant on *The Amazing Race* (we were under contract not to tell anyone but our immediate families about the race), I took a leave of absence from my legislative correspondent's position. I did not worry about an income. After all, I planned to win the million dollar prize!

In November, I left to take part in the "classified" race adventure, and United States Congressman DeMint became United States Senator DeMint! When filming wrapped up, I was able to arrive home a few days before Christmas; I was tired, excited, and now single as I was no longer dating my teammate from *The Amazing Race*. A few days later, Scott called to ask me to go to dinner on my birthday, December 27, 2004; it would be just he and I—no other singles hanging around! After that night, we began to date exclusively and became the "talk" of the little old church ladies!

A year later, I returned from India just a few days before Christmas. Scott was out of town visiting his Mississippi family for the holiday. I shared a lot over the phone with him, but I felt relieved he would be coming home on my birthday and our "dating anniversary," so I could share my biggest story with him . . . the call I had to adopt.

He arrived in town around lunchtime on the 27th. We had planned to spend the day together, as he needed to leave for a mission trip the next day to Louisiana to help with Hurricane Katrina Relief. I wasn't nervous about telling Scott about God's call for me to adopt one day. Scott and I had already discussed adoption in general, because he had been adopted domestically as a baby. He felt fortunate to have been chosen by his parents. Adoption had been a wonderful, loving experience for him and his adopted sister, Stephanie, because they were genuinely welcomed into their immediate family.

We went to his house so he could unpack from his Mississippi Christmas trip and then re-pack for his mission trip to Louisiana. He listened to me rattle on and on about my trip. I confided in him about the way God had silenced my ears to hear my call to adopt and how I recognized God was leading me to adopt someday; Scott, supportive and kind, listened intently to me. Later he told me he didn't realize how serious I was about adopting at that moment, but he knew if we were married and it ever happened, he would be a great father to an adoptive child because of his own experiences.

Scott says, "When I was growing up, I often received questions about what it was like to be adopted. Other kids simply did not understand. They would ask questions like 'Do you know your real parents?' To which I replied, 'Yes, I live with them.' To me, the mother and father that were raising me WERE my real parents. In addition, other kids often seemed to feel sorry for me; I never really understood that sentiment. On the contrary, adoption made me feel significant because I knew my parents saw me and chose me. The main reason I could face tough questions with confidence and never felt a sense of inadequacy was in large part due to my mother. She spoke with me about my adoption before I was even able to understand it. She always spoke in a way that made me valued."

Finished with packing, Scott told me he needed to make a quick stop at the church to get some van keys for his mission trip the next day before we honored our reservations at the fancy restaurant he had booked to celebrate my birthday and our dating anniversary in style. Then, right before we headed to the church, he gave me my "combination" birthday and Christmas gift bag filled with books, magnets, and plaques about couples and marriage. I didn't get the hint. I just said, "Oh, how nice! Thanks!"

When we arrived at the church, we entered the foyer of the church. I turned to go toward the church office area, but Scott grabbed my hand and pulled me instead toward the sanctuary. I was confused since we were there to get the van keys. I thought to myself, *how strange; they keep the keys to van in the sanctuary*? It still had not dawned on me what he was up to.

We stepped into the sanctuary. There were candles glowing on the altar and flower petals on the floor. Suddenly I realized what was going on . . . he was going to propose! As he pulled me toward the altar, I was so surprised, I vividly remember laughing giddily and nervously.

Scott handed me a Bible with my soon-to-be-married-name engraved on it . . . *Kelly Parkison*. I opened the Bible with my trembling hands and found a beautiful diamond ring inside the Book of Ruth. I remember Scott's hands were shaking as well as he knelt on one knee. Although I can't recall each word he said to me, I do remember him saying, "Kelly, you would make me the happiest man in the world if you will marry me."

Of course, I responded with a joyful but nervous "Yes!" To my surprise, someone else called out, "Congratulations!" The couple

Scott recruited to pre-light the candles and toss the petals for him had hidden nearby and appeared around the corner. There was no way Scott could deny being a romantic softie now! His man-card might be in danger!

My romantic sweetheart had thoughtfully arranged for my family and some of my extended family to be at my parents' house after he proposed so we could all celebrate together before our dinner. That was special to me because he alone orchestrated all of these little details. I was able to show off my new ring and share this joy with them.

We left for our celebratory dinner, adding our engagement to the list of noteworthy events to observe on December 27th each year. Scott had generously arranged a fine-dining experience at *The Chop House* to honor this special event. (Afterwards he said, rather begrudgingly, he had wasted our money; all I had done during the entire meal was excitedly plan a wedding and didn't even notice the fantastic food!)

The whole day was storybook perfect, but I had one more unforgettable memory from that incredible day. Scott secretly learned how to sing and to play Keith Urban's "Memories of Us." After dinner, back at his house—soon to be **our** home—he serenaded me with the song as he played the guitar. I knew beginning my life with him could not get here fast enough!

We were married in our church five months later on May 6, 2006. We honeymooned at a Sandals Resort in Antigua with some of my winnings from *The Amazing Race*! Much to our surprise, a few months later, three pregnancy tests later, and a doctor's visit later, we digested the news that we were expecting our first child. Our son,

Seth Austin Parkison, was born on May 20, 2007, just a few weeks after our first anniversary.

Watching Scott transform from husband to Daddy in one instant was such a beautiful sight. I fell even more in love with Scott as he cradled and spoke tenderly to our newborn son. He was a natural at being a father, and he was going "pro" right from the start. He even changed the first poopy diaper at the hospital!

Soon after Seth was born, Scott was called to his first senior pastorate position in Wakefield, North Carolina; we moved five hours away from my family, our Greenville home, and our Taylors church home. We were transforming and building our own little family.

Life drastically changed for us in those fifteen months, but I had never forgotten India. I left part of my heart in that country and still felt connected to it. I often pulled out my pictures and re-read the stories I had written in a journal. I certainly had not forgotten God's call to me. Not that I am anything like Jesus' mother, Mary, but the Bible says when the angel told Mary she would be mother to the Savior of the world, she *pondered* all of these things in her heart. I guess, like Mary, I too was pondering the words God had spoken. I constantly reflected on the image of a small Indian girl and held in my thoughts the plans for more trips to India.

When I dwell on something so much, I talk about it a lot. Just here and there, I dropped little hints or made comments to Scott, but for the most part I clung to the hope that Scott would soon resolve to pursue this dream with me. The anticipation was causing me to grow impatient.

Our new church in North Carolina was very interested in doing missions in Africa, and as pastor, Scott was supportive of this idea. However, because there appeared to be little interest in doing missions in India, I was disappointed, especially since a couple was called out of this church to serve in *India* before we ever came on staff! Of course, I was crazy about Africa when we were visiting there during the race; I often wished I could return to that continent. However, when mission trips were being planned, it was as if my heart's compass always pointed me toward India.

Scott departed to South Africa with the church team. They had a rewarding trip and accomplished their goal of leading people to Jesus.

A few months later, we were invited to an incredible conference on missions in Virginia, Impact Your World. I knew the importance of spreading the gospel worldwide, but after this conference, I became even more impassioned for India.

At this conference, we learned two new terms regarding foreign missions: "unreached people groups" and "unengaged people groups" (UUPG). Unreached people groups are a population where less than two percent are evangelical Christians. The term unengaged people groups is used to refer to a situation in which there are no evangelical church planting efforts being implemented. In laymen's terms, unreached people groups may have a missionary or a church present, but there is still a low percentage of believers; a people group is considered unengaged when they have no access to the gospel and there are no missionaries or churches trying to reach them.[4]

---

4 "Unengaged, Unreached." Global Research, International Mission Board, Web. June 28, 2015, http://public.imb.org/globalresearch/Pages/MapUUPGs.aspx.

Once again, as I write them, the words *no access* jump out at me. During one of the lectures, the speaker displayed a huge map of the world, and on the map were these tiny, different-colored dots. The colored dots represented various people groups all over the world; however, it was the red dots that held my interest. The red dots were representative of unreached and unengaged people groups in the world. I was heartbroken when I saw the highest concentration of these red dots was in India.

In America we pass churches on almost every corner as we drive around. We have Christian radio and television programs and mobile phone apps to give us spiritual inspiration. We stay in a hotel and find a Bible in the nightstand. We ask strangers in America if they know Jesus and most could tell us something about Him even if they do not believe in Him.

Continuing to look closely at that map, I could see some red dots in almost every country, but there was one country literally covered in red dots: India. After seeing the countless red dots, my desire was fueled even more to participate in mission work there as soon as possible. My heart was locked in for good!

I immediately grabbed Scott's arm and pointed out the numerous red dots. I said, "Look up there. Do you see which country is covered in red? It's India!" I hoped to spur him toward seeing India's urgent need of the gospel. He had already conceded that God had been urging him to set his ministry focus more toward finding unreached and unengaged people groups somewhere, and he was currently praying about where God wanted him to go. I was thrilled I might soon get my wish.

Well, Scott did follow God's urging, and a few months later, he headed to the Amazon on another mission trip to a UUPG. *What? Why not to India, God?* I was reluctantly supportive of this trip since doing missions anywhere is worthy, but I so wanted us to be like-minded in our passions. Selfishly, I believed if Scott went to India, he would want to adopt from there as well. I began to wonder if, deep down, Scott was unsure about adoption. Could that be the reason he seemed resistant to go to India?

Because I can be persistent and stubborn and like to believe I'm right about everything, I became more determined than ever to open Scott's eyes to mission work in India. I pondered this notion often and prayed fervently and without ceasing for God to change Scott's heart and mind.

Speaking of change, we were still considered newlyweds, but the only constant we were experiencing at this point in our marriage was change. Just as we showed signs of adapting to marriage, having a dog and a son, moving away and undertaking a new position in a new church, we became pregnant with our second child! Our little Levi, actually not so little by birth weight (8 lbs. 11 oz.) was born on a snowy day in January 2009 in Raleigh, North Carolina. We had added another beautiful baby boy to our family, and God was blessing us.

Before Levi was born, Scott had wondered if he would be able to love a second child as much as he loved Seth, our firstborn. When we met Levi, Scott and I realized we had plenty of room in our hearts to love this child too. We fell deeply in love with little Levi Scott Parkison.

Shortly after Levi was born, I brought up the idea of adoption—frequently. Early in our dating relationship, Scott and I had discussed and even downright argued about how many children we might have if and when we married. I had always dreamed of having a very large family. As a child, I decided I wanted to have seven kids so I could be like the Captain von Trapp family from the musical, *Sound of Music*! However, in my teens, I lowered my desired number of children from seven kids to five kids. Perhaps I changed my mind because I had started babysitting more and realized I might not be able to handle seven!

At any rate, Scott argued with me that two kids were plenty. We could not come to an agreement—or at least Scott would not agree with me about this. I considered not dating him anymore because of it. We decided to end our on-going argument and compromised on three children; Scott promised perhaps later he would be open to the possibility of considering more than three children. He says he knows better now; he should never give me any leeway or possibility, or I will make it happen and get my way!

After Levi was born, I knew it was time to not only ponder the possibility but to start talking seriously about adoption. If we adopted, it would give us our third child and fit into our little family plan and agreement. Scott wasn't sure how he truly felt about it, but he gave me the go-ahead to at least look into it and research it and get some more information for him to consider later.

Well, that was all I needed! After that conversation, I spent hours looking up information, trying to find anything online about India's adoption procedures. Unfortunately, I didn't find much information, but I did find a website that stated a couple adopting from India should be married five years. We were getting close to our three-year anniversary, so I reluctantly calmed down and relaxed a little bit and just continued to pray to God to change Scott. Time was forcing me to wait.

In the meantime, after commiting his decision to prayer, Scott determined our church should take a mission trip to India in order to visit the Russells,[5] the couple who had been called out of our church to serve with the International Mission Board (IMB) in India. Now I had these two small boys—Seth was two-and-a-half years old, and Levi would turn one year old right before the trip dates—but I desperately wanted to return to India.

I especially wanted to be there to see and experience it with Scott on his first trip there. It was a tough decision for me, especially as the trip got closer. In the past, Scott and I never really worried about what could possibly happen to us during times we traveled together. But now, responsible for two children and traveling at the same time, we chose to establish a Living Will for the both of us. It seemed so frightening to me; drafting those wills made me think God placed that notion in our hearts because we were going to die! Everything seemed so final. I struggled with leaving the boys. I continued to pray, and I wrote this in a blog post on our family blog:

> The Lord has taught me a great lesson in obedience while preparing for this trip to India. I knew when I first heard there would be a potential mission trip to India I needed to go and wanted to go. I sought the Lord in prayer and definitely felt His affirmation to go. But now as the trip approaches, I have two small children to consider as well.

---

5 Name changed for security purposes.

I didn't know the struggle I would feel inside about being away from them. It's true Seth has spent some time away from me for two weeks before and we are only going to be gone 17 days on this trip. Levi has been away for one week from us without any problems. So, I would think I could handle it.

But there seems to be something that feels so final or just so far away about going to India that it has created this internal struggle in my heart.

Well, the Lord has been working on me about obedience . . . the very thing I work on with my children :) I know He wants me to go, so I need to trust Him.

The Lord calmed me as He spoke through this Scripture:

> *Anyone who loves their father or mother more than me is not*
> *worthy of me;*
>
> *Anyone who loves their son or daughter more than me is not*
> *worthy of me.*
>
> ~Matt. 10:37, NIV

I was allowing thoughts of losing my children to almost consume me . . . basically like an idol. I do love my Savior more than my children. And guess what . . . He loves my children more than I do!

So, all of this to say . . . I realized when I let go and gave my children over to Him, everything was going to be okay, regardless of what may happen to me.

I felt such a freedom, although I admit it was hard to get to this place. I had faith, but I confess I cried so hard when they pulled out of the driveway today with my parents, but I now have a peace, a peace they will be okay because they belong to the Heavenly Father and not me. And besides, I know I will see them again soon. If not at the RDU airport in 17 days, they can find me one day at the banquet table in heaven. I'll be sitting at the table that serves Indian food!

So we left for India with a team of four others, trusting God and realizing being a parent changes everything, although it changed us in a great way! It challenged our faith and our obedience, and our children were with us in our hearts the whole time.

As we landed in India, I made sure to watch Scott's face and reactions. As the familiar odors hit my nostrils, I grabbed his hand and said, "Welcome to India!" It was very late at night so somewhat quieter when we landed in New Delhi; we would have a very short stay there as the next flight to Jaipur would be in the morning. Scott's reaction to the traffic was about the same as mine. Our taxi driver happened to go the wrong way on a one-way street, and I heard Scott yell out, "Whoa!" nervously. The next day he would experience a little more culture shock when he could actually see everything happening around him.

He took it all in like a champ. I was proud and excited to experience this with him as well as with our group from church. We were impressed with the ministry happening in Jaipur, with the Russells, and with the new Indian brothers in Christ we were meeting. Jaipur was a great experience, but our team was also traveling south to Bangalore to visit an orphanage where one of our team members had a connection.

I was "super psyched" about this because this could be the day God placed a desire to adopt in Scott's heart! Anytime Scott made a comment about how precious the children were, I would quickly chime in with "Don't you want one?" and "If we adopted, we could have one of our own." It sounded like I was picking out a pet, but it was my way of making light of the subject while clearly presenting my heart's desire. I knew he was getting the message loud and clear from me; I hoped God was sending him the message too. Bangalore was a special time of doing both ministry and loving on orphans. What a privilege for us to visit there!

After Bangalore, Scott and I went to Chennai for a few days to visit the Gupta family, the family with the fifteen adopted girls I had met previously during my media mission trip. I was thankful Scott was interested in seeing how this family had affected me and to see the very place where I felt and heard the call to adopt.

Four-and-a-half years had passed since I met the girls, and I was amazed at how much they had grown up. They still had their musical talents and serenaded us with a few of their harmonious songs. The house was still full of love and joy, and it was a wonderful time of visiting with old friends. I asked the Guptas if they thought I would be able to adopt from India, but, regretfully, they told me they thought it would be very difficult. They said adopting out of country, especially girls, was neither common nor easy to do.

Our visit to India was everything and more than I could have prayed for. First of all, I was extremely relieved we didn't die as I thought we would! Secondly, Scott enjoyed our experiences there, and we both came away with even more love and enthusiasm for missions and for India. And lastly, two of our team members felt called to serve full-time at Jaipur with the IMB. Scott and I also considered serving overseas full-time, but we did not get peace about that decision.

There was something stirring in our lives though. Not long after returning home, Scott resigned from pastoring in Wakefield, and we were called to Trinity Baptist Church in Manchester, Tennessee. We packed up and moved to Tennessee with our children and earthly possessions; of course, my passion for adoption and the country of India came too!

Chapter 3

THE CONVERSATION

AFTER RETURNING FROM OUR TRIP and moving to Tennessee, we began to educate ourselves about the entire international adoption process. We still did not meet India's requirements for prospective adoptive parents to be married for at least five years. This gave us another year to pray, research, and gather information. God used radio and online sermons and Scriptures to confirm the calling I had in my heart.

To my astonishment, one day on Facebook I came across a high school friend, Jennie Cornwall, who had recently adopted from India. She gave me an account of her journey through adoption, sharing crucial information and lessons learned from her personal experience. What good news to discover she had been allowed to adopt a child from India when she already had three other biological children! Having four children was working out just fine for her. This planted a huge seed of hope in my heart and mind. I voiced this conclusion to myself: "The Guptas told me it might be more difficult to adopt internationally from India, but if one family can do it, so can we!" I didn't miss the fact Jennie was successfully raising four children, either.

We were focusing on our new church and acclimating ourselves to Tennessee life, but in the back of my mind I eagerly anticipated our five-year anniversary approaching in May. I could no longer keep my thoughts and dreams about the adoption to myself, and I constantly bombarded Scott with the research and information I came across. I also mentioned—more than a few times—how I would welcome having another baby of our own; I'm sure I was pretty annoying as I continued trying to convince Scott to take the next step to officially and legally start our adoption process.

Out of nowhere, Scott said it seemed I had forgotten about our mutual acceptance of "The Policy of Joint Agreement" negotiated right after our marriage. This policy idea came from a book written by Willard F. Harley entitled *Your Love and Marriage*[6]; Scott had read this book in 2000 and discovered this policy years prior to our marriage; he had been swayed by its truth and requested we put it into place in our newlywed home. I had agreed.

The reason Scott had determined we needed to adopt the policy? A week or so after we returned from our honeymoon, since we were childless, I decided we needed a puppy to be our "baby." I grew up having dogs as pets and wanted one for our new little family. We weren't expecting yet, so it seemed like a good idea to me. Scott had been single for about fourteen years and hadn't been a pet owner for quite some time. Because we didn't have a fence, it would need to be an indoor dog. He wasn't thrilled about the idea and actually said several times that he didn't want a dog and we weren't getting one.

Nonetheless, I can be very persistent, persuasive, and stubborn, and after all, we were still in our honeymoon stage. Scott, doing his

---

6 Harley, Willard F. *Your Love and Marriage*, Baker Books, Grand Rapids, MI. 1997, page 17.

best to please his new wife, at last agreed to a dog. Even though he totally denied it and still will, Scott loved our little Yorkie named Samson, even though from time to time Samson would irritate the fire out of Scott. Just as Scott would get comfortable, Samson would scratch to sleep in our bed or to get on the couch. I must also admit that I was not good at housetraining Samson, and many accidents happened. When this occurred, Scott would not only get angry with Samson but also with me because, in his mind, it was my fault—I had "forced" him to get this new puppy.

After the dog issues caused so much tension, Scott decided to introduce the "Policy of Joint Agreement" to our marriage. Basically the policy states that one person alone cannot influence a major decision that would affect the family financially, emotionally, or physically. Both parties would have to be in *enthusiastic* agreement for something major to happen or to change in the family. It had been easy for me to agree to this policy; after all, I still had Samson!

That conflict easily resolved, Scott resigned himself to the fact his bachelor pad and man cave had been invaded by a dog (our "first baby") and by me, but at least he had established the "Policy of Joint Agreement," and we should live happily ever after. (As a side note, Samson lived with us for five more years but currently lives with my 87-year-old grandfather, who needed a companion when his dog died. We still get to visit our "first baby" when we visit my Papa Walter.)

I share the reasons behind our family policy because, as I continued to annoy Scott concerning officially opening the adoption process and hinting for another child, he pointed out that I was breaking the sacred "Policy of Joint Agreement." I was ignoring our mutual agreement to have only three children total if we did adopt. This was a source of contention, but please understand we were not combative or openly argumentative with each other.

I want to be clear Scott was not against adoption. As I mentioned before, he had a wonderful experience of his own, but he was adamant: we had agreed we were going to have only three children total. He firmly said I was going to have to decide, one or the other . . . adoption or biological. He reminded me of the policy, declaring, "We agreed!"[7]

As a woman, I struggled with my desire to birth another child. I still had a deep yearning within me to get pregnant again. Yet I knew, without a shadow of doubt, God clearly had called me to adopt from India. At the same time, it was hard for me to dismiss my childhood dreams of having a large family. Why did it have to be one or the other? Why could it not be both?

To avoid distress or anger over Scott's ultimatum, I began to hold fast to the idea that Scott would eventually come around to see it my way. Surely I could make him change his mind. I did my best to explain in some subtle and some not-so-subtle ways why we should adopt *and* have a baby too. I would have podcasts about adoption playing aloud while he was in the room, or I would inform him of couples I knew who were adopting and had large families. I made comments about how the Scriptures talked about large families being a blessing.

It was clear he knew how I felt about the situation, but it was clear to me how he felt as well. Secretly, I began to resent Scott for the choice he was forcing me to make.

Fervently and ironically, I began to pray for God to make my pastor husband more spiritual . . . like me, of course! (Ha!) This is the

---

7 Ibid.

same man I saw daily reading his Bible and praying and pouring out his heart to his Heavenly Father; I saw him working and providing for our family while caring at all hours of the day or night for members of our church family; I saw him constantly being an incredible daddy to our two sons. I decided Scott's lack of desire to adopt and have another baby too was a spiritual issue . . . perhaps he didn't love God as much as I did.

Just putting those thoughts on paper is hysterical and embarrassing, but that is what I resolved it to be in my heart. Oh, the hypocrisy on my part! Thankfully, I was convicted of that mindset and came around. I knew my husband had a deep, deep love for God and the Word and that he is way more spiritual than I am.

I didn't believe one decision over the other was more spiritual, but they both felt "right" and spiritual to me. I knew the love I felt for my biological children, and I knew I had a deep desire to have another one. But I knew as well that I was distinctly called by God to adopt, and I felt I would be walking in direct disobedience to God if I did not do both.

The clock was ticking. Our five-year anniversary was almost here. A decision needed to be made. Will we have more children? Should we officially begin the adopting process? How could I make the choice? One child was not more important to me than the other. I desperately wanted *both*.

All I could do was pray. I prayed for God to change Scott's heart. Scott, at times, patiently listened to my pleas, but I could see he was still adamant about us choosing one or the other. I began praying for God to put us on the same page, to give Scott a stronger desire to adopt and to be willing to have a third biological child. I wanted God to confirm to Scott He was directing us to do this.

In May of 2011, we celebrated five years of an awesome marriage. To celebrate, Scott and I took a cruise to the Caribbean. The cruise and its excursions were a special time for us to be alone without our two children and to focus on each other. We swam with dolphins, sang karaoke tunes, danced, and laughed a lot. We enjoyed being with each other. It gave us a chance to reflect on all that God had brought us through in our marriage and our ministry together.

Redirecting the focus of my marriage, it was during this anniversary time that God took hold of my heart and convicted me about my attitude toward my husband. Even though I knew Scott was very wise and seeking the Lord about this matter, I still held on to a little resentment in my heart. It hurt that he was making me decide. I felt alone. Regardless, I was not alone; God had been with me and with our family throughout our lives, and especially in the past five years. I could sense how much my husband loved me. It's not like he loved me more on the trip than before, but I think the blinders and the barriers I was putting up came off, and I could see just how blessed I was to be married to this incredible man.

The last night on the ship, I decided to spend some quiet time with the Lord. On that very windy night, I made my way up to the very top on the front end of the boat, the windiest place. I chose to go there because no one would be crazy enough to sit up there due to the wind, and I would be able to be alone with God, to talk out loud to Him with no one eavesdropping. I began crying out to God, praising Him for the incredible blessings He had given me the past five years. I thanked Him for my awesome husband and for putting Scott in my life. I asked His forgiveness for my impatient and slightly bitter heart toward my husband concerning adoption and having another baby.

After spending almost a year praying for God to change Scott, I finally said, "Lord, change me! Change me to be more like you and more like my husband." The burden of worry lifted from me, and I encountered an awesome time of refreshment and renewal in the Lord!

The next day we disembarked from the ship. I felt like a new person. I had full trust in the Lord and full trust in my husband. We picked up our boys and headed home.

During the drive home, Scott suddenly said, "God has been working on me. I feel what you desire to do with adopting and having another biological child is a good plan. There is spiritual value in it, and I know God is speaking to you, and I want to encourage it. A true godly desire for you is also a call on me."

I was in shock and wondering to myself, is this for real? Suddenly, it hit me like a brick—all this time, *I* had been the stumbling block. I thought it was Scott who needed to change, but it was *me*! I needed to change *my* attitude. God showed me *He* was the one in control, not me. In HIS perfect timing, He orchestrated this.

Looking back, I could see it all so clearly. If Scott had given in to my desires early on, without praying and pursuing God's will, he might have resented me if any problem arose with the adoption or with having more than three children. I might have resented him too, as I already had proven I would do, for not being on board about having four kids. I would have continued to feel alone and to isolate myself from him, which in the long run would have affected our marriage and family unity. God's perfect timing is always best.

God was showing me a pattern in my behavior. Consequently, this was the second time I had wanted something so badly and tried to force it without waiting on God to lead. I became aware that if and when I gave the control to God, only then would it be in His perfect timing and work for the best.

The other situation where God taught me this truth had involved my desire to marry. Once Scott and I started dating, I knew we would more than likely get married. Scott says he knew the same thing, but he wanted a clear "go ahead" from the Lord before he asked me. After dating about nine months, I was becoming frustrated and impatient. I was impatient with Scott and more frustrated with the Lord; I liked things to happen when I wanted them to happen. To my distress, there was not much talk of marriage, and Scott reiterated to me he would not move in that direction until he had solid confirmation from the Lord.

We were on a singles Christian retreat at Montreat in Asheville with other singles from our church. I was having lunch with a friend and discussing the whole idea of marriage. She shared with me she had placed her full trust in waiting on God to bring her a husband, and she was totally cool if God wanted her to be single because she wanted to be fully in His will. Her words convicted me and challenged me.

The final night of the retreat, I hit my knees and just gave up. I gave up trying to control if and when I was to marry and who I was going to marry. I even ended my prayer of submission by saying, "God, if You want me to be single, I will. And You can be my husband."

Here comes the lesson: Days later, after Scott's proposal, he mentioned to me that God had given him the peace and affirmation to choose me for his wife while we were on that retreat; he said it had happened during his personal quiet time early in the morning on the day we were leaving the retreat. How astounding to learn that God gave Scott the "go ahead" the morning after I had earnestly released my desires to marry into God's hands. I had stood in God's way by trying to control the situation. When I gave Him the control, He could in His perfect timing work for my best interests.

Back to our conversation on the ride home from our anniversary cruise . . .

How excited we both were to be in God's will, and how exciting to be discussing our growing family! We had a lot to talk about on our ride home. We were dreaming about having four kids and wondering what she, our adopted daughter, would be like. Soon our dreaming ended as we faced reality and spent the rest of the drive planning ways to fundraise. I knew we were on our way with no stopping when Scott corrected me and told me to stop using phrases like "the little girl" or "the orphan" or "the child we will adopt" when I was referring to her. He said, "From now on, we call her **Our Daughter**."

I felt a deep, abiding love for my husband in that moment. He was already caring about her, and he was also caring for me. I was no longer alone in this situation; we were now in this together. Looking back, I am so thankful for God's perfect timing and so grateful I never moved ahead without Scott's full support. The journey we were about to embark on was going to be crazy; it would be difficult; it would test us. I would need Scott to be there for me whole-heartedly. I could have never survived our journey without him or Him.

EEEK! We were going to be parents again, but this time to an Indian girl. For the past five years we had discussed adoption, gathering information and asking ourselves important questions: What would it mean for our family? What would it mean for our boys? What would it mean for us financially? What would it mean for our church? What would it mean for our extended family? Why adopt from India? Will we have more biological children?

WHAT WOULD IT MEAN FOR OUR FAMILY?

When a family has chosen to adopt, they embark on an incredible journey that will make them jump for joy and yet want to rip their guts out at the same time. I had listened to podcasts and read some insightful blogs and had prepared myself for the possibility that our family could face serious hardships on this journey. I was aware adopting another child could lead to some major changes in the family that could affect the birth order of our biological children and affect our emotions, our finances, or our stability if our adopted child had special needs, opening a whole new world of potential challenges for us.

I was and still am a fighter. When facing problems, one principle my family instilled in me was never to quit and never give up. Forge ahead! I struggled in school with learning disabilities, and while it was difficult to be successful in school, dealing with it helped me develop perseverance. I taught myself to keep going with all that I had within. In addition, I have read in Scriptures and seen it play out in my life during the good and the bad, my almighty God always gets the glory! The Bible didn't promise this life would be easy; in fact, it is full of Scriptures that speak of quite the opposite.

The book of James tells us to consider it joy when tough situations arise. That became my thought process for this potential adoption journey. I was prepared for it to be hard, but I would push through the challenges. I knew my little family could persevere as well; most importantly, since God indeed had called us to do this, He would be with us through it all.

I had no doubt Scott and I could be great parents for our adopted child. I don't mean that in a boastful way, because we are not perfect. Our parenting is still a work-in-progress, but our life experiences had been preparing us for this decision. Scott, adopted himself, could easily relate to our child, and it gave me assurance to know if our child ever struggled with abandonment or feeling different from our family, she could go to him to talk about her feelings and their shared experience. Besides his personal adoption experience, he had proven to be an exceptional father to our two boys, and I knew his love would have no limits with an adopted child.

As for me, I had learned in my life that bloodlines and DNA had nothing to do with family and nothing to do with love. I grew up in a blended family, and I understood what it meant to be unconditionally loved by someone without being blood related. My family never saw and observed titles like *stepfather, stepdaughter,* or *half-sister.* We were just family.

In addition, Scott and I understood, through the love we had received from our Heavenly Father, that unconditional love had nothing to do with bloodlines. We had both experienced a spiritual adoption in which we recognized Jesus Christ came and died upon a cross so we could become a part of the family of God.

Now you are no longer a slave but God's own child. And since you are his child, God has made you his heir (Gal. 4:7, NLT).

Now if we are children, then we are heirs—heirs of God and co-heirs with Christ, if indeed we share in his sufferings in order that we may also share in his glory (Rom. 8:17, NIV).

So that, having been justified by his grace, we might become heirs having the hope of eternal life (Titus 3:7, NIV).

WHAT WOULD IT MEAN FOR OUR BOYS?

Scott and I both considered what adoption might mean for the boys, and we came to the conclusion the adoption wouldn't be harmful to them but would instead lead them to develop a stronger godly character within them as young men one day. Whether we adopted or had a child biologically, they would learn to be protective, loving big brothers. The adoption process would give us more teachable moments for our boys.

Because adoption is a living and in-color picture of God's love for the human race, the boys would have a front row seat to experiencing this concept. In addition, they could be exposed to the hardships of orphans and potentially see the blessed lives we have as Americans compared to the rest of the world. We knew this experience would stretch all of us, especially our little boys, as they would have to share their parents with a child who might be needier at times. We prayed these things would teach them firsthand about being selfless, about loving others more than themselves. I could see a possible "win-win" for the boys!

WHAT WOULD IT MEAN FINANCIALLY FOR OUR FAMILY?

International adoption is very expensive. In fact, I think the costs often scare people away. From our estimations, we were going to need about $30,000 to get our daughter from India and to cover all of our expenses. It was a daunting task, but I was up for the challenge. Since God called us to action, He would be with us. We believed He was in charge of all of our possessions and not just the ten percent we tithed.

Most of my professional working experiences involved fund-raising. For the past ten years of my young adult life, God had been preparing me for this season! I sold ad pages and raised money for charities during my participation in the Miss South Carolina/Miss America Pageants; as a college intern, I worked as an event planner at the Chamber of Commerce in North Myrtle Beach; I handled public relations while serving as a legislative correspondent in Washington, D.C.; as the Associate Director of Alumni Affairs for North Greenville University, I planned and hosted events for the alumni and raised funds for the school; additionally, I solicited donations to raise money for my mission trips. God had spent years preparing me for this daunting task of raising $30,000.

Due to God's perfect timing and intervention, our family finances were in decent shape. We were not rich with money to spare, but we had what we needed. The Lord had brought us to a church with a parsonage, so we did not have a mortgage; therefore, we were able to save money and use it toward school loans and other debts. We also finally sold our home in North Carolina, and our eyes were opened to see God was taking the worries out of our family finances to allow us to concentrate on raising money for our adoption expenses.

WHAT WOULD IT MEAN FOR OUR CHURCH?

This was probably the only question I could not fully answer. I knew we had no control over what people would think of our adoption and whether or not they would support it. But knowing my church family and how loving they were to Seth and Levi, I expected we would get a positive response. I decided having an adopted child would not be different for them because she would be another one of the preacher's kids, and she would be loved on just the same as Seth and Levi.

I believe adoption can positively affect churches by exposing them to the needs and hardships of orphans, by encouraging pro-life efforts, and by inspiring other families in the church to pursue adoption as well. What a difference the body of Christ can make in the global orphan crisis if we all work together! Statistical data revealed if one family in every three churches in the United States adopted a waiting child, every waiting child in the United States would have a forever family.[8]

WHAT WOULD IT MEAN FOR OUR EXTENDED FAMILY?

Again, believe it or not, I couldn't predict what everyone in our family would think about the adoption. Our families had always been supportive of us, so we expected they would support us in this endeavor as well. We love our families so much and think they are awesome, so it was exciting to grow our family number even more.

WHY ADOPT FROM INDIA?

We were also not naïve to the fact some folks might question why we would adopt from India when there are orphaned children right here in America and why we were choosing to adopt a girl. We already had the simple answer prepared: God said so. So what that we

8 Abbafund, "Adoption Assistance for Christian Families," Adoption Facts, accessed June 30, 2015, http://abbafund.org/adoption-journey/adoption-facts/.

could still have kids biologically? So what that our daughter might have a different skin color or have special needs? It didn't matter in reality what others might think about our desire to give an Indian daughter a valued place in our family. It mattered only that we followed God's will and His call.

WILL WE HAVE MORE BIOLOGICAL CHILDREN?

Well, to answer the last question . . . I answer with a resounding YES!

Chapter 4

Y'ALL ARE CRAZY!

THE TIME CAME TO MAKE our "baby announcement." We were nervous to share the exciting news we were going to be adoptive parents. We weren't quite sure how the news would be received.

Some members of our church and our friends in the community speak their minds—or voice both positive and negative opinions to us—on any issue. In addition, Scott and I both come from very vocal families who don't hold back their opinions, especially when it involves us or their grandbabies or when they disagree with our decisions.

I was not as worried about people's opinions of our adopting or even their stance on adoption as I was about the disappointment and anger I might feel toward anyone who seemed opposed to our decision. Scott would repeatedly remind me, "No one is required to be happy about this or be as excited as we are." But inside, I knew I'd be mad if someone tried to talk us out of it, and I have just enough "redneck" in me to react defensively.

If we were going to get negative feedback, it would be for one or two things:

Why adopt when we can have biological children? Why adopt internationally when we could adopt in America?

Knowing I was concerned about negative feedback, Scott encouraged me, saying, "We should not respond harshly, but answer all questions truthfully. If someone were against our adoption or discriminated against our daughter, we could not change that person; only God could change his or her heart."

These are our truthful answers to the questions we received:

WHY ADOPT WHEN WE CAN HAVE BIOLOGICAL CHILDREN?

I guess our family adopting would seem strange to some because God had already blessed us with two incredible biological children (and potentially more), because most families who adopt are people who were unable to have children, like Scott's family situation. Based on my experiences with other families who have adopted, it seems more and more people blessed with biological children are adopting as well.

Though we feel blessed to have biological children, we felt that a series of events compelling us to adopt had taken place in our lives: Scott's own adoption experience, my growing up in a super loving, blended family, and our own spiritual adoption by our Heavenly Father. Also, as we studied multiple Scriptures, listened to sermons, and heard testimonies, we felt God leading us to adopt.

God has clearly shown us His views on the importance of taking care of orphans and defending the fatherless all throughout the Bible. Psalm 10:14, 17–18, James 1:27, Jeremiah 22:16, Matthew 25:40, and Psalm 68:5–6, to name a few, reveal His truths. Needless to say, adoption has been on our hearts for a very long time.

WHY ADOPT INTERNATIONALLY WHEN
WE COULD ADOPT IN AMERICA?

There is no denial that all children need and deserve a loving home; that is God's best plan. And, please hear my heart, I am not saying international adoption is better or more spiritual than domestic adoption. It all came down to the fact that both Scott and I have a HUGE passion for India. We have loved on India in person and from across the world! Between the two of us, at publication we will have been to India fourteen times. Although India's culture, her cities, her people, and her languages vastly differ from our own, we have fallen in love with her.

Knowing now how much we love India, it makes for a great fit! We have personally met and worked with orphans in India and know firsthand there is a great need for homes and families, and more importantly, *Christian* homes for waiting children. After seeing India in person and gaining a better understanding of the world's financial system, we have seen firsthand that the poorest of the poor here in America appear wealthy compared to most of the people in India. In fact, the American poverty line for daily earning, which is $29.85, is more than 20 times higher than the poverty line for daily earning in India, which is $1.25.[9]

In India, most orphans, especially girls, are fighting to survive. Most of them are picked up and placed into some sort of slave trade, whether it is sex trafficking or slave labor. Most of the children who are begging on the streets are collecting that money and then having to turn it in—for lack of a better word—to a pimp. They barely receive enough funds to survive, making them dependent on their captors or bosses.[10]

---

9 Donovan Preddy, "Poverty Comparison: India vs USA," *Design Impact,* 2013, http://issuu.com/d-impact/docs/us_india_final/1.

10 Paloma Sharma, "A Marriage of Inconvenience," *Justice for Women* (blog), April 17, 2013, https://justiceforwomenindia.wordpress.com/tag/trafficking-statistics-in-india/.

Females in India are fighting a different battle altogether. Because most females are aborted, if they survive in utero, then they are lucky to survive their first few years without being murdered by a parent or grandparent. Girls are considered a curse, mainly because of the dowry system set in place for marriage. Even though it is now illegal to take a dowry, it is very much a part of the caste system of India and a part of the system of arranged marriages [11]

These reasons are also why we chose to adopt a girl from India instead of a boy. Because India is more receptive to letting you adopt outside of your current gender of your children, having our two boys gave us a better chance to adopt a girl. I have already mentioned the Gupta family taught me the importance of adopting orphaned girls. It was there I learned orphan girls have a much more difficult time making it on the streets than orphan boys. It was then that the seed was planted in my heart to adopt an Indian girl one day.

To sum up our answers, we know God confirmed this call through years of prayer and Scripture reading. This is what we were supposed to do . . . our daughter was there, and we needed to bring her home!

I'm grateful we received mostly positive feedback and encouragement. We did observe some strange looks and were asked lots of questions. One or two gave us no response at all, which led me to think they were apathetic or perhaps disapproved; as I predicted, it angered me, but I held onto my composure. Sometimes I have to remember I'm a pastor's wife!

I couldn't help but wonder how they would have responded if I told them I was pregnant versus telling them I was adopting. I'm sure

---

11 Soutik Biswas, "How India Treats its Women," *BBC News,* December 29, 2012, http://www.bbc.com/news/world-asia-india-20863860.

I would have received at least a word of congratulations. I wanted others to know our adopted daughter would be our child too. She had not yet arrived, but I was already feeling the need to advocate for her and defend her. The concept was just bizarre to some people, it seemed.

I was most worried about how to tell my family and how they would react to it. Well, my toddler, Seth, helped me out with that. He broke the ice in a rather comical way. While my family was visiting in the parsonage, Scott and I had to run an errand. Apparently, Seth intently listened to our conversations more than I knew and tucked them away in his little mind, because while we were gone, he announced to my parents and sister, "Guess what? I'm going to get a little sister from India!"

When we entered the parsonage, my mom slyly glanced up and asked, "So, you guys are adopting from India?"

I laughed and said, "How do you know that?"

She said, "Seth let the cat out of the bag!"

We all started laughing, and my parents declared they were happy for us and excited to get a new grandchild and gave us a hug. Then we sat and told them all about it.

I was so thankful Seth had simply laid it out there for us; it took some pressure off of us trying to find a way to share the news. After that, it felt easier, so we called and e-mailed other family members and let them know about our new addition coming to the family. The majority of responses were full of congratulations and statements of how they couldn't wait to meet her.

Although supportive, I knew our parents had genuine concerns about the financial aspect of this process—especially when we explained the expenses involved. They didn't want to see us go deeply in debt. Because they loved Seth and Levi so much, they worried about the changes the boys would face. We just reassured them that God was in control and that we had to be obedient to His command to adopt.

Our friends were supportive as well. Some of them expressed how wonderful we were to do this for a child, especially when we had children of our own, and how lucky our daughter would be. They meant well, but Scott and I were not seeking praise. We certainly were not the heroes in the storyline. All the glory should be directed to God for His love for our daughter-to-be and how He had arranged this whole situation. No, we weren't the heroes, but He was! Our response was "We will be the lucky ones to have her in our lives one day."

Even knowing God was in control, I developed a nagging fear that our daughter might be treated differently, not cruelly, but as someone less important than our biological children. My fears stem from my husband's experience with his adoption. Scott's immediate family loved and accepted him unconditionally, but he admitted there were times he felt like an outsider among lesser-known extended family. He grew up without negative feelings about being adopted, and he and I pledged to do our best to make sure our daughter never felt unloved or devalued.

In my own blended family, we all went out of our way to blur the bloodlines. We treated each other as if we had been together from day one. That was to be our plan for our daughter too.

I was eleven years old when Mom and Eddie Cisson married. I affectionately called him "Coach Eddie;" it's the name my brother Brent and I gave him when they were dating, because he coached at the high school.

I remember that one evening I was working on a homework project before Coach Eddie came home from practice. The assignment was to trace the history of our family tree by interviewing both our parents and putting each of their family ancestors on the proper tree branch. I listed Coach Eddie on the "Father" side of the tree, but he was at football practice, and I figured my mom couldn't tell me the Cisson names I needed. I called Nanny, Coach Eddie's mother, and asked her to give me the names I needed to finish my homework, but she wouldn't. Instead, Nanny tried to encourage me to use only my "real" dad's family names to avoid offending his family. She said it wouldn't be right to use the Cisson name on my homework because Cisson was not my real family tree and I might get a bad grade. What she didn't realize, of course, was that she unintentionally made this little sixth grade girl believe Nanny didn't want me to be a part of the Cisson family. Nanny was trying to be respectful of my bio dad's family, but I needed acceptance and encouragement.

Coach Eddie arrived home to find me all teary and emotional. Mom explained the reason and tried to console me, assuring me it was okay and Nanny surely didn't mean any harm. I will never forget the look on Coach Eddie's face as he sprinted to the phone, saying it certainly was not okay; he called his mom, my nanny, to tell her how she had hurt me. Coach Eddie defended my choice to put him on my family tree by saying, "I am married, and this is my new family." He said *Cisson* was his name too, and Cisson blood ran in his veins. He added that my brother Brent and I would be a part of the Cisson family because he wanted us to, and it was his name to give. He reminded Nanny, "The Cisson blood does not run through your veins. You only became a Cisson yourself when you received the Cisson name in marriage. Brent and Kelly came into the Cisson family through marriage like you did. Mom, we are all Cisson family."

Looking back, that remains one of the best arguments I've read or heard applied to the acceptance of non-biological children into families.

My poor Nanny! She felt horrible and apologized to me and, of course, I forgave her. Nanny always let me know how much she loved me and how she had always wanted a granddaughter and I was to be her first granddaughter. Deep down, she only meant to teach me to be respectful of my other dad and grandparents. She also did not want me to get a bad grade if the teacher decided I didn't follow the directions. She never meant it to hurt me because she was proud to have me call her "Nanny." She soon sat with me and gave me the full rundown of her Cisson/Youngblood family history. Those were some of the most fascinating stories I ever heard. As an adult, I actually know more about my extended/blended family than I do about my own biological extended family. I even have Cisson family keepsakes and pictures I treasure.

About a year later, my little sister Courtney was born to Coach Eddie and Mom. Our blended family grew, and her birth strengthened our Cisson family bond even more. I finally had a sister. Although Nanny was especially thrilled about baby Courtney, she reminded me that I was her *first* granddaughter.

My Coach Eddie, Nanny, and the Cisson/Youngblood extended family from all over South Carolina are family to Brent and me, as they have demonstrated God's unconditional love and acceptance to us. They laid the very foundation for me to be drawn towards adoption by demonstrating what it was like to love someone not from the same bloodline. Coach Eddie taught me the definition of family; it is not only people who are blood-related but also people who love and respect and fight for each other.

Because of Scott's and my experiences growing up, I knew we would defend our daughter as Coach Eddie defended me, to protect her from any unintentional hurts or any cruel, purposeful discrimination.

As soon as we spread the word we would be adopting, we decided to go ahead and work toward having our third biological child. We knew it could possibly take up to two years or more for our adopted daughter to arrive, so we would have some time to adjust to a new baby while waiting for the adoption to proceed.

We started our adoption paperwork in late May 2011. In August, we found out we were expecting our third child to be born the following April. We were thrilled to know our family of four could expand to six in just a couple of years.

We announced right away we were pregnant because I was sick, sick, sick and couldn't hide it! I would have to run out of the church to vomit many times, and people started putting two and two together and pretty much figured out I was pregnant!

After the official announcement about our upcoming pregnancy, people constantly asked if we would continue with our plans to adopt. Others would say, "Wow! Four children is a lot. Can you afford to have four children?" Having been a pastor's wife for a few years, I was used to living our lives in a fishbowl.

Instead of taking offense, I realized people were entitled to their opinions. Those desiring a large family are in the minority these days, as it seems most couples believe two children are enough. But I disagree. The Bible says, "Behold, children are a heritage from the Lord, the fruit of the womb a reward. Like arrows in the hand of a warrior, are the children of one's youth. Blessed is the man who fills his quiver with them" (Ps. 127:3–5a, ESV).

On a side note, it dumbfounded me to find that a Gallup poll stated the ideal size for an American family was 2.5 children.[12] I'm still wondering how families would have half a child ideally! Ha!

Most people were curious and asked questions out of genuine concern; they cared about us. There were a few, though, who were determined to tell us what to do or not do. With my husband's encouragement and the Holy Spirit chiseling away at my Christian character, I truly had the power to refrain from anger.

There are numerous blogs, videos, and articles on the Internet by parents who have been involved in the adoption process. Many point to the lack of sensitivity displayed by people questioning families regarding their adoption experiences. I could certainly relate to how parents feel when people ask questions without thinking about how their comments and questions come across. I literally laughed out loud at some of the blogs and videos because they shared experiences so similar to my own.

For those considering adoption, I advise not taking offense at negative reactions to your plans; we should live our lives for an audience of One and not be so easily entangled in the snares of discouragement. We serve a God who created us and has plans for our lives that are so much better than we can imagine and definitely more than others can imagine for us.

---

12 Joseph Carroll, "Americans: 2.5 Children is 'Ideal' Family Size," *Americas*, June 26, 2007, http://www.gallup.com/poll/27973/americans-25-children-ideal-family-size.aspx.

Therefore, since we are surrounded by such a great cloud of witnesses, let us throw off everything that hinders and the sin that so easily entangles. And let us run with perseverance the race marked out for us, fixing our eyes on Jesus, the pioneer and perfecter of faith. For the joy set before him he endured the cross, scorning its shame, and sat down at the right hand of the throne of God. Consider him who endured such opposition from sinners, so that you will not grow weary and lose heart (Heb. 12:1–3, NIV).

For we are God's handiwork, created in Christ Jesus to do good works, which God prepared in advance for us to do (Eph. 2:10, NIV).

Like our lives, the adoption process is much like a race. Actually it's more like a marathon. We must have the perseverance to keep going, and not just to keep going but to remain godly and joyful even when we feel like we may be under attack. We can rest and know that we have been created to do this good work of adoption. We don't have to grow weary and tired. We have the help of the One who has "been there" and endured more than we ever can, and He desires to hold our hand, walk beside us, and even carry us through this process if we will allow Him to.

Looking back, I know those questions from friends, families, and church members were small compared to what was coming. Their questions were insignificant compared to the hardships the next two years would bring.

However, we were very blessed. While everyone had questions for us, they were also supportive and excited for us. They were praying fervently for us and encouraging me through Scripture. At a crucial time during our adoption, my friend Renea came and gave me a promise from God's Word. It would become the Scripture I ran to the most in the latter half of our adoption.

> *And blessed is she who believed that there would be a fulfillment*
> *of what was spoken to her from the Lord* (Luke 1:45, ESV).

I held tightly to this promise. When God spoke to me in the Gupta home in India, I knew His promise would be fulfilled. I just didn't know when!

Particularly from our church family, we received support, encouragement, donations, and most of all prayer. Member after member and Sunday after Sunday, they asked how we were doing and whether we had any adoption news. We could feel the love.

I would be remiss if I did not tell you about a group of women who went the extra mile. They were to me what Aaron and Hur were to Moses when the nation of Israel faced the armies of Amalek. When Moses held up his hands, the Israelites prevailed; when he lowered his hands, the Amalek army would prevail in battle. Moses grew weary and could hardly hold up his hands, so Aaron and Hur came to him and held his arms up for him until the battle was completed.

These women held me up until the adoption was completed. In times of weariness, when I began to lose faith, when I had urges to give up, when negativity would arise, these women held up my hands and lifted my chin toward Almighty God. What a blessing to be surrounded by such godly women!

Surprisingly, social media brought an abundance of support. I discovered several groups on Facebook as well as message boards full of families who were either in the process or had completed their adoptions. I even found groups that were specifically adopting from

India. They provided a lot of information for our questions pertaining to the adoption. Later on, social media and message boards would play a vital role in our story.

Using Facebook, I joined a group of moms who were using my same adoption agency. Some of these moms I have met; others, I have not. Even though our journeys are a little different, we could share openly with each other without judgment, as we have all walked in each other's shoes in some fashion. I gained a core group of friends who are still important to me. All of the original members of the group currently have their children. We continue supporting and praying for each other as we work on bonding with our adopted children, drawing them into our families, and raising them to be godly, successful, quality people.

So, while it was scary to announce our adoption plans, and even tough to accept some of the reactions, this process brought forth beauty from my family, church, community, and strangers I met only online. It was the beauty of God's unconditional love and promise that He "will not leave you as orphans" (John 14:18a, ESV).

He cares so deeply for us. He gave us what we needed, whether it was tough responses to sharpen us or Aarons and Hurs to uphold us. The whole thing was a beautiful mess that deepened family bonds and friendships and even developed new friendships.

Our family bond would grow even stronger when *Katy Pierce Parkison* was born to us on April 4, 2012. What a thrill to hold our newborn daughter in our arms while we held another daughter across the world in our hearts. Katy Pierce's "big" little brothers welcomed her wearing their "I'm the Big Brother" shirts; they were as proud of their baby sister as Scott and I were. I was already envisioning frilly little pink dresses, hair bows and braiding, ballet classes and tiaras!

Scott was already thinking of her as his Sweet Baby and as a Daddy's Girl. Things couldn't have been brighter! It wouldn't be long before things would get crazier and God would show us He has a real sense of humor!

With our family plan of four kids in place, Scott was scheduled to have a vasectomy. Then, to everyone's astonishment—especially Scott's and mine—about three months after Katy Pierce was born, we found out we were expecting AGAIN! We laughed, but only after we completely got over the initial shock. Of course we had heard of people becoming pregnant during their adoption process, but we never heard of someone getting pregnant twice.

We were due to have another baby boy in May of 2013. Scott said this last baby was an unexpected gift from God. We had planned and agreed on only four children. Because God was sending us another baby, perhaps He didn't care much for our particular "Policy of Joint Agreement"![13] Ha! This was our journey with God and a part of His divine plan and our preparation.

Poor Scott! He had been so concerned about having four children, and now we were going to have five. *Joel Edward Parkison* would arrive May 22, 2013. I smile as I recall my Mom teasingly saying to Scott, "You let Kelly have her way!"

Five children . . . ready or not!

---

13 Harley, Willard F. *Your Love and Marriage*, Baker Books, Grand Rapids, MI, 1997, page 17.

Chapter 5

SHOW ME THE MONEY

SCOTT AND I HAD A plan when we started the adoption paperwork seeking approval: I would be in charge of all the fundraising, and he would do all of the paperwork. I don't really know that one is easier than the other. To raise $30,000 is daunting, but then the amount of paperwork and following the exact procedures can be overwhelming as well. We're talking about a five-inch stack of paper signed in the right places, notarized in the right places, and initialed in the right places. I was positive I got the better end of the deal.

As I mentioned, God had been preparing me for this task of fundraising all along. While a college student, I interned with the Chamber of Commerce in North Myrtle Beach, working as an event planner. Later, competing in the Miss South Carolina Pageant prepared me as a spokesperson and an advocate.

After the pageant, I worked in Washington, D.C., for Congressman Jim DeMint. Here I was exposed to the world of politics and legal paperwork, and I observed and learned a good bit about event planning. When I left D.C. and became the Associate Director of Alumni Affairs for North Greenville University, part of my job was to plan fundraising events and to solicit monies for donation and use various resources I learned from my mass communications degree.

I was mentored by some of the best at North Greenville University. The school had seen its share of hard times, but with strong leaders unwavering in their faith, North Greenville University had a complete turn around at a time when the trustees were ready to close its doors. Now the school has 2,451 students and includes a graduate program.[14] Some of those leaders and professors were still at North Greenville when I was there, and I was able to observe and learn from them. While I was employed there, I learned to be obedient to God's direction and trust that He would provide for the call; to strive to have the funds in place and never go in debt over a vision or a plan; and to surround oneself with a strong support team.

In addition, one thing became clear throughout my various fundraising experiences. I am much more comfortable asking for money for a cause or a charity than asking for donations for me personally. I admitted I'm better at event planning for fundraising than I am at straight up asking for contributions.

So there I was, in a fundraising role once again, and it caused me discomfort. I needed to do the very thing I am not good at: seek money or donations for what I believed was a personal cause. One could argue this money was for the greater good of our daughter and the plight of orphans. But the truth is people were helping my family adopt a child when we already had children of our own. I believed it was a personal mission, since God called me and later called Scott to expand our family in this way. It was very personal! However, God

---

14 North Greenville University, "NGU Welcomes 19th Consecutive Record Enrollment," accessed July 2, 2015, http://www.ngu.edu/ngu-welcomes-19th-consecutive-record-enr.php.

would teach me how He would support me and solicit funds Himself by speaking to the hearts of others in our path.

Have I mentioned that I'm a fighter? As uncomfortable as I felt asking for money for something so personal, I was up for the challenge. Everything I had been reading in Scripture and listening to in the podcasts reminded me to have faith and trust that God would help me by providing every penny.

In all honesty, money was the biggest roadblock we faced in meeting the requirements. Scott worried we would be unable to raise all of the funds needed, and he did not want to go into debt over the adoption. Scripture warns against debt, and Scott had worked hard with our budgets and finances to be as debt-free as possible.

The total cost needed at this point was $23,000 to cover the adoption fees. An additional $7,000 would cover travel and extra outside expenses accrued during the process. Our main goal was to raise the $23,000 to take care of the actual adoption costs. Then we agreed we would try to personally absorb the additional $7,000 cost ourselves. But, God had bigger plans, as is often the case!

Our agent presented us with our payment plan broken down into three segments. Once our first deposit was made to the agency, we would be able to begin the paperwork to officially start our process. We would have a payment due to Janet at Holsten Homes to cover the home study expense in addition to the agency payment. After that, we would make two more payments until we were paid in full. There was no deadline for the payments.

The payment process could go as fast or as slow as one would like. Of course, we were in a hurry to get our daughter. After all, I had been waiting on her for five years already! Scott told me we needed to raise $13,000 to move forward to the second step in our adoption process. So, I decided to set the goal of raising $13,000 by October. We were in May, so I had five months to raise the money.

Scott was doubtful and feared my disappointment if I failed to reach my goal. I, on the other hand, had no doubt it could be done. I loved the challenge, and I had full faith that, when God called me to adopt, He would not leave me alone in the process. I knew He would show up and provide. I never seriously worried about the money part of it.

I wanted to keep people informed of our progress and to tell them how they could pray for us. I planned to create a blog that could have a second purpose of keeping track of my funds as they accumulated. I had begun a blog about five years earlier to keep the family updated about the various things going on in our lives. That blog soon became an online baby book for us, documenting many milestones and great stories about our children. It had allowed us to stay connected to our extended families. Starting a special adoption blog would be like having a baby-book for our daughter-to-be, and it would be an efficient way to document her beginnings with us.

It was difficult to create a name for the blog. I wanted it to be just right. I petitioned my family and a few friends to help me come up with a creative title. My family, in typical fashion, mostly came up with funny names and things associated with a play on words, such as "*Sari*, This Was All I Could Come Up With" or "You Had Me at *Namaste.*" (Namaste translates to hello). However, a church member and good friend, Janet Galyen, came up with the perfect title. She knew God had continuously used the first seven verses from Isaiah 43 to draw me to adoption. The verses are as follows:

But now thus says the LORD, he who created you, O Jacob, he who formed you, O Israel: "Fear not, for I have redeemed you; I have called you by name, you are mine. When you pass through the waters, I will be with you; and through the rivers, they shall not overwhelm you; when you walk through fire you shall not be burned, and the flame shall not consume you. For I am the LORD your God, the Holy One of Israel, your Savior. I give Egypt as your ransom, Cush and Seba in exchange for you. Because you are precious in my eyes, and honored, and I love you, I give men in return for you, peoples in exchange for your life. Fear not, for I am with you; I will bring your offspring from the east, and from the west I will gather you. I will say to the north, Give up, and to the south, Do not withhold; bring my sons from afar and my daughters from the end of the earth, everyone who is called by my name, whom I created for my glory, whom I formed and made" (Is. 43:1–7, ESV).

These verses inspired me through the call and through the journey to adoption because they painted a beautiful word picture of the spiritual adoption that takes place between Father God and His children. He has redeemed us, called us by name, and we are His. He is with us when life is hard and will not allow anything to overtake us. He gives in exchange for us. He desires us to be His sons and His daughters.

In the same way, this is how I felt about my unknown daughter. I desired her to be with our family. I longed to take care of her. I wanted her to know she was mine, a part of the Parkison family, and no one could take that away from her. I was willing to give, exchange, and sacrifice for her to be a part of our family.

I am not God; I don't have the capability to love and sacrifice the way He has for the world. But God revealed that as much as I already loved my daughter, He loved her that way too and loves her more than I do. It brought me comfort to claim these Scriptures over her because I knew God already knew who she was and had claimed her as His child. He already knew her name. And so my friend Janet gave me the blog title "**Heknowshername.blogspot.com**."

My first blog post was on May 23, 2011. It included a pretty picture with a caption that read: *"My child, you may not know me, but I know everything about you."*

> *"O Lord, you have examined my heart and you know every-thing about me"* (Ps. 139:1, The Living Bible).

I wrote, "Scott and I are pleased to announce we are in the beginning process of adopting our daughter from India. We don't know who she is, how old she is, what she looks like, or her name . . . But God does! We cannot wait to meet her! We love her already!"

I knew in my gut, without a shadow of doubt, God knew exactly who was going to become a Parkison girl, and it brought me great comfort to know He knew everything about her past. He knew what was to come!

May 23rd happened to be the day we received our first "donation." The first $2,000 came from my nanny, Annette Cisson. She was no longer with us on earth, but years prior, without our knowledge, she had purchased her grandchildren a savings bond that matured in 2011. When my parents surprised me with the bond, Coach Eddie reminded me Nanny would want me to use it wisely and to put it toward something valuable. Scott and I could think of nothing more valuable than the life of our daughter. It brought me great joy to know my daughter's great-grandmother had invested in her unknowingly, and one day I would get to tell my daughter all about Nanny and that she was the first to give! A few days later, my brother Brent and his wife Emily, after receiving his bond as well, sent part of his gift to me too. Amazing love.

Starting our fundraising off with $2,000 right away gave me more confidence that God was going to provide what we needed! He already showed up and surprised us with $2,000 we didn't know about—in the form of a secret savings bond—He is so cool like that! And then that amount had been increased with my brother's contribution. Our child was being loved and valued from the start.

In a donation section on my blog, I added a tool to measure our money. It was a thermometer for displaying our money totals as we received online donations or as we recorded totals raised during our events. Our thermometer was proof of God's provision! We have long-distance family and friends who couldn't attend our events; this made it easier for them to participate. The thermometer was just a fun visual to let everyone watch God work! The thermometer showed our $13,000-by-October goal and that we had less than five months to achieve it.

The blog was not just about the money; it also functioned as spiritual therapy for me. It gave me a chance to tell our story, ask for prayer, and record our thoughts and happenings. It helped me not to feel alone. I recalled blogs written by adoptive parents, which helped me in my journey during that first five years of contemplating and praying. I hoped my blog would function as an instrument of hope and a resource for another family thinking about adoption as well.

In one of my early posts, called "It's Not Just Money We Need," I wrote:

> We really need your prayers! This whole process started over 5 years ago and has been bathed in prayer and it won't stop now! The cool thing is . . . this has basically been a prayer for Scott and me only. We are so pumped to think about the hundreds of friends and family members joining in prayers with us!
>
> This process is long and I hear unnerving . . . It is amazing to me how much I already love my daughter. I often dream of her and wonder about her future. I pray for her . . . just like I did the whole time I was pregnant with the boys. Although we know nothing about her at this point, I have already started worrying . . . just like a Momma! Is she already born? Is her birth mom getting proper care? Is she being treated well in her orphanage? Is anybody loving on her tonight? Has she even been held? God please show her you care . . . send your angels to sing to her. Tell her she has a Mommy and a Daddy, and two brothers that love her so much!
>
> So, all of that to say . . . it is hard to wait and wonder. I am constantly reminding myself of Scriptures that speak of waiting and sitting still. If you know me . . . that's hard for me to do. Especially when I have a goal in mind! Please pray for me . . . I need patience. I am reminding myself to enjoy this season I am in right now. Thank you in advance for your prayers!

While actively planning fundraising events, I would use the blog to announce them to the community. We started with our first event, "The Hamburger Plate Sale," at the Gospel Festival in Manchester. In my opinion, Scott is awesome on the grill, and everyone who has ever eaten one of his burgers loves them! Many people in our church rallied behind us and donated food items and baked goods and volunteered their time to help us with the sale.

There was one small obstacle that day—the weather. The weather was horrendous. Rain poured down from black skies, but we continued to press on and kept grilling. Our friends were willing to get soaked to support our cause. Then, Levi slipped on a wet sidewalk and busted his head open; I had to leave to take him to the ER for stitches.

Despite the forces that seemed to be against us that day, we raised $800! I was blown away! God was so good to us on a day that seemed so stressful.

In addition to hamburger sales, I held two fundraising beauty pageants in my home state of South Carolina, and Janet, who named our blog, rode with me to help. Others showed up to help too. At one of our pageants in Greenville, Janet's brother, a local television weather personality, gave up his day off to help us man the table. My sister Courtney came from Columbia to assist with the little contestants. I was very grateful to Jeanna Rainey Beasley, a former Miss South Carolina, who came from Charleston to direct and emcee. In fact, Jeanna had been instrumental in suggesting this event as a fundraiser to me. This particularly touched my heart as she had struggled with trying to have a baby and had miscarried five times, yet was unselfishly coming to help me.

Other events we held were talent shows, family photography sessions, manners camps, and garage sales. We had a group of over thirty friends who volunteered their time at a *Warrior Dash* event in the community. Each event required much planning and preparation, but each one was worth it. The events became a time of fellowship for us with our friends, and at each event we received a blessing financially, spiritually, and emotionally. We were grateful to all of those in our church family who donated food, money, crafts, supplies, and most importantly their time as they volunteered to help plan our events, babysit our boys, and provide us with physical labor and supplies, which they did with no expectations in return.

One generous soul donated all the hamburger meat when he heard of our hamburger sales, and our friends, the Hambys, jumped right in as the events rolled around. We were uplifted by the love and support of all of our friends and how much they already cared for our daughter. There were so many people who made these events successful. Even if their names are not mentioned here, God knows who they are.

Using our blog to solicit donations required less work on my part but was a much more stressful experience. I would blog about our needs, update our thermometer, and then post and wait. I would wait to see who God encouraged to give. I would be fearful no one would give, fearful we were bothering someone with our request, or fearful someone would give out of obligation.

Scott and I wrote a letter together to mail. After we sent it out, God started using what seemed so hard and uncomfortable to challenge me in my spiritual walk as one of His disciples. God wanted me to understand patience. Waiting is such a huge component of the adoption process. I was unaware at the time, but in retrospect, all the waiting and hoping for our finances to come through was preparing me for the hardest part of the process—waiting on my child.

Waiting has not been a strong suit of mine. I have always been a goer, a doer, and a planner. I want things to happen when I want them to happen. God confronted me directly with a lesson on patience and "being still" during one of my pageant fundraising weekends. I blogged about it in this way:

> Well, all last week my quiet times were pumping me up and I just knew God was going to do this huge thing and provide us with tons of money through the pageants for the adoption. Saturday morning my quiet time devotional asked a question at the end . . .

"Are you willing to wait on my blessing?"

I didn't like reading that question because I am not good at waiting and I had my hopes on God providing tons of money through the pageant fundraisers and meeting my goal right away.

Please hear me say . . . $2,500 is a lot of money, but if almost everyone that asked for information about the pageant had competed, we could have raised around $8,000-$10,000. I just had my heart set on that amount of money.

So after two successful pageants, I was feeling a little discouraged because I did not quite raise as much as I had hoped I would, but I still felt great. I mean $2,500 is still a big chunk, and it is a huge help! But then God did something even bigger than I could have imagined . . .

While I was home in South Carolina during the event, several of my family members handed me checks for the adoption. One check was for $1,000, and five more were for $100 each. I was stunned. I had not even thought about God providing through my own family this weekend.

As I returned to Tennessee, I found taped to my back door a card from a dear friend at church. I thought it was a sympathy card because my grandmother had just passed away while I was home. I opened the card, and there was another $1,000 check. So over the weekend another $2,500 was raised!

The next time my devotional asks, *"Are you willing to wait on my blessing?"* I will answer with an enthusiastic "**YES!!!**"

After we sent out over 500 letters and e-mails that contained our petition for prayer and financial support, God started showing up in a phenomenal way. The coolest part for me was witnessing the people who were not even on our radar who were led to give. I don't know why we were so surprised because we know God can use the unlikely to do His work. I was astonished by the generosity of so many of our friends and family. Their generosity was not just a blessing; it was also a spiritual challenge to me to open my eyes to how I could be more generous to our family, friends, and community as well.

Another sweet story was when two precious little sisters in our church, Emily and Kaylee, donated $20 from a lemonade sale they held in their neighborhood. Their mom made a comment about how it wasn't that much, but it was huge to me. These sweet girls gave all they had. They could have used it to buy a new toy, some candy, or some ice cream, but instead they gave it to help our family. It was a sweet sacrifice on their part and another example of godly generosity.

More checks continued to make their way to our mailbox, evidence of family members, friends, and even strangers donating to help us. People wrote cards with their donations, telling us of God's prompting in their hearts to give to us. I was just blown away.

I was at a loss for words when we met our goal of $13,000 a month earlier than planned. Scott admitted he thought there was no way in the world we were going to meet that goal that soon. However, that number had some major significance to me, and reaching it early was important to me; as soon as we met that goal, it meant we could move forward to the next step of our adoption: the dossier and a referral. I blogged about it, of course!

> I shared our financial goal with some friends, and we laughed about how I never aim for anything small and how it would be okay if that goal wasn't reached. It would happen in time, and I just needed to trust God. There were even a few nay-sayers . . . Scott being one of them.

> Well, I love dreaming God-sized dreams, because God answers in God-sized ways! It is the last day of September, and the goal was not only reached, but exceeded! I say "we did it!" Not because it was anything that Scott and I did, but first and foremost, God did some amazing things. Then God used tons of our friends and family to give and donate to us generously . . . whether it was time or money.

> I just have to share a few things . . .

> There have been a few fundraisers that I personally worked on thinking these will be large money makers for the adoption . . . and they did not turn out as well as I thought. But God would just drop some opportunities in our lap to raise money, or people would send us a check in the mail saying God had laid us on their hearts.

I just want to shout out at the top of my lungs! I praise you, Lord, for the great things you have done! Great are the works of your hands, and great are your people!

Then I want to scream a huge thank you to all of our friends and family that have helped us in so many ways! Donating items for hamburger sales, garage sales, monetary donations, and for volunteering time at some of our events. And most of all, for the prayer and love!

Now, because we have exceeded $13,000, we heard from our agency that we can proceed to the next step in adoption—the dossier, and then the referral. We are closer to knowing who our daughter is!

And, my husband just wrapped his arms around me and humbly admitted that he should have known from the beginning I was going to accomplish my goal! It feels good to be right!

As exciting as reaching that goal was, the fundraising didn't stop there. We still had a long way to go! We hosted more events, and generous donations continued to flow our way. God continued to show His grace and His provision. One sweet way we saw God's provision demonstrated was at Christmas through a Sunday school class in our church. The ladies collected $500 and gave it to our adoption fund. It was a humbling, tearful moment for me, as I saw my church body coming around us to support us.

Scott and I had applied for a grant for our adoption. Some good friends told us about an incredible organization called the JSC Foundation. We wrote the required grant essay and sent it along with

Pregnant at the Taj Mahal on the trip we got the grant

the financial records and documentation from our agency in hopes of being awarded a grant.

Shortly after Christmas, Scott and I and six others from our church left to do missions in India. Here we were in the same country as our child, yet we had no clue where she was. Every sweet little face I saw, I couldn't help but wonder, where is she?

On New Year's Eve in India, we completed a day of work with the missionaries, ate supper, and headed to bed. Before going to sleep, I decided to check e-mails to see if we had news from our kids at home. And there it was, an e-mail from the JSC Foundation. It was so surreal to be sitting in India with drums pounding from a wedding party going on outside our window. The e-mail from the foundation gave us incredible news. While this mission trip had nothing to do with our adoption of our daughter, it was crazy we were in her country when we received this news. We had been awarded a $13,000 grant for our adoption. This completed the rest of any monies due and would also help with our travel to get her when the time came. Scott and I immediately jumped up and started dancing down the hall of our hotel to the Indian drums and music, and of course we had to run to share it with the mission team!

We serve an awesome God who deserves all the praise! When He calls us to do something, He takes care of us! We have seen this over and over again in our adoption process, and once again He took it a step farther by providing travel expenses for us. I mean—wow!!! We were in shock and kept re-reading the e-mail to make sure we read it right. To God be the glory, great things He has done!!!

Yep, $13,000!!! I cry even as I write about this three years later. God had a bigger plan all along. He did not allow us to use one penny of our own finances, not even for the travel. He gave it all to us—to our daughter and to our family! Keep in mind as well, this was all done before we even had a referral. We did not know who she was!

But we remembered, *He knows her name!*

Chapter 6

PAPERWORK PREGNANCY

PAPERWORK PREGNANCY **IS A PHRASE** used in adoption circles to represent how adoptive parents occupy their time prior to the arrival of the child. I was never one for paperwork. I didn't enjoy writing papers in high school or college; organization is definitely not my best suit. One reason I have loved blogging, even though it is writing, is that it's written in "Kelly Format," not MLA, APA, or Turabian. "Kelly Format" consists of misspelled words, run-on sentences, sentence fragments, misused commas, an overdose of the words *that* and *so* and *feel,* and an excessive use of ellipses. But thankfully, Scott and I had made a deal; he would handle the paperwork and I would handle the fundraising. It wasn't like our deal was exclusive; we both helped each other along as we could. He would be present, promoting, and volunteering at our fundraisers, and I, of course, would assist with research, give input on essays, and be involved when he needed the extra help. Thank you, Lord, that Scott did most of the paperwork!

In fact, he did so much of the paperwork I could not always converse on the topic with other adopting families. They would ask, "So where are you with your I-800 papers?" or "How is your dossier coming along?" Often I couldn't answer because I had no clue. I couldn't even pronounce or spell the word dossier. To me, when pronounced correctly, it sounded like a fancy French word for a piece of furniture. Again, I am very grateful Scott assumed that burden.

When we first started our application requirements, we wanted to hear firsthand stories about the paperwork aspect of international adoption from other families. One evening, we met for dinner with the Starrs, who had adopted from South Korea, and another time we spoke with the Millers, who had adopted from both the Philippines and Vietnam. Each family had their own unique story and experience, especially the Millers, as they had to deal with paperwork rules and regulations from two separate countries. One common theme we heard, not only from these families but from others as well, was the overwhelming amount of paperwork involved in an international adoption. It was massive and mind-blowing. A quote from a t-shirt I saw on Pinterest explains it best: "So far no morning sickness, but the paper cuts are terrible."

Paperwork pregnancy consisted of mounds and mounds of data to be turned in at various times and to various organizations throughout the process of waiting on approval. The main brunt of the paperwork went toward completing the dossier. Aside from the dossier, there was massive paperwork to be accomplished for the required home study and for U.S. Immigration. Hopeful parents would work their fingers to the bone and lose sleep in order to complete the paperwork in the quickest manner possible.

An adopting parent orders, pays for, and produces a ridiculous amount of original birth certificates for each member of the family.

They gather birth and marriage certificates along with tax records, financial records, medical records, and clean criminal records. It's the most comprehensive background check and information gathering on an entire family that you could imagine, and it's compiled in a document about the size of a ream of paper.

There are so many agencies and organizations intertwined in this dossier. It was not completing the forms that was extensive; it was all the gathering and assimilating of all the information. Our background checks had to be gathered from every state in which we had lived. We had to retrieve multiple birth certificates, and at that time, three out of the four of us were born in different states! We had to go to the local sheriff's office for a local background check. We went to the health department and were tested for HIV and TB. We had to have specific medical forms filled out by our physicians and pediatrician. We were fingerprinted by the Tennessee Bureau of Investigation. We had to write our life story in an essay. We had to re-quest and then retrieve and sort recommendation letters from people. The list seemed endless!

There were so many organizations involved in this process that would review all of this paperwork, organizations such as the USCIS (United States Citizenship and Immigration Services), the FBI, our home study agent, and our adoption agency. In India, we dealt with the Indian Government, SARA (Stateside Indian government), CARA (Central Adoption Resource Agency), and the India Judicial System. The whole process was mind-boggling and is perhaps one of the rea-sons adoptions move slowly; but on the other hand, I was relieved both governments go to great lengths to make sure children get into safe and qualified homes.

In addition, all this paperwork is assembled in a hurry-up-and-wait order. Adopting parents work tirelessly to complete the paperwork because in our minds it means our children will arrive here more quickly. If a parent took their sweet time finishing, it could delay things to an even greater extent. Our mindset was that if we get it done faster, our daughter would be here sooner. This I did not consider: our paperwork would be turned in and then left in others' hands; it might sit on someone's desk for quite a while, or it could be in line behind many other families involved in their own paperwork nightmare. But even in retrospect, we would not have done it differently. We still would have busted our tails to get it done. I couldn't imagine prolonging the process any more than necessary on our part, and completing the dossier and submitting it gave us a slight sense of control over the process.

In her blogpost, "The Truth about Adoption: One Year Later," Jen Hatmaker refers to this part of the application for approval. She writes, "Here is the upside: This is the stage you realize God can put a vicious fight in you for a kid without your blood coursing through his veins. Those early doubts about loving a child without the helpful instincts of biology are put to rest. Of course, you don't know this kid yet, but you love him in your heart, in your bones. You'll fight like [anything] to get to him. You can't think of anything else. You are obsessed. You dream about him like you did when you were pregnant. You realize that when God said He sets the lonely in families, He meant it, and He doesn't just transform the 'lonely' but also the 'families.' He changes us for one another. God can create a family across countries, beyond genetics, through impossible circumstances, and past reason."[15]

---

15 Jen Hatmaker, "The Truth About Adoption: One Year Later" *Jen Hatmaker* (blog), August 21, 2012, http://jenhatmaker.com/blog/2012/08/21/the-truth-about-adoption-one-year-later.

The end made the work worth it. God was transforming us, making us into better parents, not only for our adopted child but also for our biological children. It was tough, time-consuming, and just plain awful sometimes. But when the paperwork on our end was over and we heaved a great sigh of relief, the most difficult part was about to begin. We would look back and think, "Wow! That paperwork was easy stuff compared to this."

My organized husband handled our paperwork like a pro. The paperwork had to be the most mundane part of the process, and he knocked it out! When we had the go-ahead, he had the home study, the dossier, and the I-800 completed and turned in within a month. That's right, that's what I said: a month. He worked on it every day, and it still took a month, and that's just one portion of it, but thankfully the largest part of it was completed. Our adoption agent, Lori Bollemen, was also helpful too, as she mentored Scott as he completed each step. He told me he did not fret over the paperwork; he would just complete each step and move on to the next one as Lori had recommended. I was so proud of him and very grateful I did not have to deal with this directly!

We were so appreciative of our home study agent, Janet Jenkins, who prepared us for this chore. In fact, I need to back up and tell a "God Story." Yes, a God Story. Only He could have orchestrated some of the people and events He placed in our lives; it was certainly not by our doing or knowledge. We saw evidence God was even assisting us with the paperwork!

After five years of thinking about and researching adoption and prayerfully considering who we would use as our agency, the next decision and first step in the process was completing our home study.

Island Coast International, our adoption agency, required us to use someone for the home study from within our state of residence; in addition, they had to be Hague-accredited or affiliated with writing Hague home studies.

According to the United States State Department website, the Hague Convention is an international agreement to safeguard inter-country adoptions and establish international standards of practices. It also establishes safeguards to ensure that inter-country adoptions take place in the best interests of the child. There are 92 countries as-sociated with the Hague Convention. If a family adopts from one of these countries, the Hague policies and procedures must be followed.[16]

We discovered India is considered a Hague country, so we were re-quired to have a Hague-accredited social worker for our home study. I researched the Internet to find one in Tennessee. There were a handful of them, so to simplify my task, I picked the home study agency with the cheapest fees. Holston Homes was about $500 cheaper than the rest. But God was not only helping us save money; He was giving us a gift as well.

When I contacted the social worker, Janet at Holston Homes in Chattanooga, for information, I knew immediately this was the case-worker we needed. Janet had adopted two daughters from India; it was another confirmation God was placing the right people in our path.

Janet's adoptions had taken place over fifteen years earlier, but knowing she could walk us through the process and give us any input we needed was comforting. Janet gave us spot-on advice as we com-pleted our home study with her, and though technically not part of

---

16 U.S. Bureau of Consular Affairs, *Hague Convention*, accessed June 28, 2015, http://travel.state.gov/content/adoptionsabroad/en/hague-con-vention.html.

her job, she advised us through some of our other paperwork phases as well.

According to www.adoptuskids.org, the home study is a written document a caseworker writes about an adoptive family and includes basic information drawn from interviews with family members and information provided by third parties. Generally, a home study includes the following: family background, statements and references; education and employment; relationships and social life; daily life routines; parenting experiences; details about the home and neighborhood; readiness and reasons as to why wanting to adopt; and approval and recommendation of children the family could best parent. The home study process takes between three to six months to complete. The findings determine whether a family is eligible to adopt, and includes the age range and number of children a family desires along with the conditions and characteristics of the children they request.[17]

I struggled internally with the last part of the home study. It felt demoralizing to list our preferences, as if adopting a child was as simple as shopping for a new shirt. Nevertheless, it is a part of the process, and a family would be shrewd to follow the guidance given by a caseworker.

Although our intentions were to adopt one child having minor correctable special needs, Janet advised us to state in our study we were open to adopting multiple children and children with severe special needs. She recommended this because in her professional experiences, some families create parameters that are too narrow, only to change their minds later in the process. For example, a family

17 "Completing an Adoption Home Study," *Adopt US Kids,* accessed July 3, 2015, http://www.adoptuskids.org/for-families/how-to-adopt/completing-an-adoption-home-study.

may complete a home study stating they intend to only adopt one child but later change their minds and want to accept a referral for multiple children or for a child with special needs. This results in a prolonged process in which the home study would have to be resubmitted, causing major delays in their adoption process.

We agreed with her wholeheartedly; we did not want to have any unnecessary delays. Therefore, our home study report officially stated we were open to multiple children, up to four actually, and we would be open to children with special needs. In some international adoptions, a child may be labeled as a special-needs child due to age or a condition. The condition could be as minor as an extra digit, a cleft palate, or a lazy eye. There are many children of the world with severe physical, developmental, or mental special needs, and I am so thankful God calls so many families to adopt those incredible children!

Our home study had been initiated in mid-June of 2011, and we completed it in early November at the same time Scott completed our dossier. Now that we had met the requirements to move to the next step, we received our first referral in December. The referral is when the agency sends information about an available child with a picture, if possible.

This particular referral is still tough for me to write about. We received a referral for sisters, two precious sisters. Originally, Lori sent the referral to Scott alone. He wisely requested he be the one to receive all referrals; Scott knew I would say yes to any child that came across our computer screen, and he did not want me to get emotionally attached until we could decide together what was best for our family. He hesitated to tell me about these two little girls, but finally he decided to mention them.

I quickly e-mailed Lori and asked her to send me the pictures of the girls. When I received the e-mail, I took a deep breath and opened it up. There were two precious faces staring back at me, Manjeet and Maduh[18], whom I affectionately nicknamed "M and M." The correspondence listed the girls' birthdates, but no other information was present in the e-mail. Scott's assumption of my response to this referral was correct; I immediately was ready to say "yes." My only qualm? We would be adopting two girls instead of one. Two girls who were so close in age to our sons wasn't what we had planned . . . but how could we say "no"?

I sensed Scott was skeptical since he didn't want to tell me about them in the first place. His hesitation had more to do with adopting more than one child because we were already expecting our daughter, Katy Pierce. He was overwhelmed thinking about the idea of parenting five children. In addition, he had some concerns about Manjeet, the oldest, being so close in age to our firstborn son. Seth would be only a few months older. We had previously discussed long before we had received this referral the need to keep Seth as the oldest in the birth order. We just knew Seth and how a change would have affected his personality. He definitely needed to remain the leader.

Conflicted, I called my Mom and told her about the girls. I fully expected she would talk some sense into me and tell me it would be too hard and too tough; she would side with Scott. But surprisingly, she seemed to be neutral and stated she would be supportive no matter what we decided. She finished our conversation saying she knew Scott and I would follow God's guidance.

---

18   Names changed for security purposes.

Scott and I took some time to pray separately about it. When we came back together to discuss Manjeet and Maduh, the conversation was very difficult and emotional. I could see I was not the only one struggling emotionally with the decision; Scott was wrestling with it as well. Everything in his reasoning and in his practicality was telling him this was not right for our family. Regardless, he still felt spiritually and physically responsible for those girls. We had been to India; we had read articles and stories about the objectionable way girls are undesired and discarded; it seemed we were teaming up with the bad guys and leaving these two without help.

I had major concerns. What if they were never adopted? For one thing, there are many more orphan girls compared to orphan boys in India. The fact that they were siblings would reduce their chances of adoption. India's policy of keeping siblings together, which is a superb policy in my opinion, would make it harder for the two of them to get adopted. After all, that was why we were not going to accept the referral. We regretfully and emotionally contacted Lori and told her no. That was tough!

Scott continued to be concerned about their spiritual wellbeing. He said to me, "I feel like I am sending them straight to hell." He was troubled they would never get to hear about Jesus and what He had done for them. We felt responsible, and we felt guilty. However, neither of us had a sense of peace about taking them as ours. It had not felt "right."

It was tough for the reasons already mentioned, but also tough because I didn't know when we would receive another referral. It could be months! It made me question whether or not I had what it took to stomach these tough decisions. I was also worried how we would know when it was "right" to accept a referral. All I could draw on at the moment was God's Word in these times of doubt:

The righteous shall live by faith (Romans 1:17b, ESV).

Now faith is confidence in what we hope for and assurance about what we do not see (Heb. 11:1, NIV).

You keep him in perfect peace, whose mind is stayed on you, because he trusts in you (Is. 26:3, ESV).

Do not be anxious about anything, but in everything by prayer and supplication, with thanksgiving let your requests be made known to God. And the peace of God, which surpasses all understanding, will guard your hearts and your minds through Christ Jesus (Phil. 4:6–7, ESV).

These were a few of the verses I went to for comfort during that tough time as we waited for another referral and worried about "M and M." We had received the referral for "M and M" in December, and from there we went into a short holding pattern. We would have to sit and wait for another referral to come our way. We still did not know who she was, where she was, or what she looked like, but God knew her name.

Speaking of names, Scott and I had decided more than likely we would give our daughter a new name. Renaming her has spiritual significance to us; in the Bible, God often renamed specific people He adopted to use for His kingdom. He would give them new and different names with significant spiritual meaning.

We read a book by Russell Moore called *Adopted for Life*. In his book, he talks about his own experience in adopting two boys from Russia and why he chose to rename his children. He wanted them to know they were his children, part of his family, and part of his American heritage. He chose their names when he became their parent, just as any new parent would choose a name for their biological child.[19] This thought process resonated with us, and we chose to rename our daughter for these same reasons. As we became her new parents, we would give her a name bearing significant spiritual meaning.

The job of naming a child is very important to us, as I am sure it is to most parents. It takes a while for us to agree on names and to settle on one. Some parents choose biblical names, while others use names starting with the same letter or pass on family names. We chose to use two criteria to name all five of our children: the first names were to be four-letter names, and the name should have some spiritual significance.

The boys' first names have four letters, and they are all named after men in the Bible: *Seth, Levi,* and eventually *Joel.* The name *Seth* means "a new beginning." In Genesis, Seth was the third son of Adam, after the debacle between Cain and Abel. I always thought it was cool that Seth began the genealogy that led to Jesus. Seth and I share the same middle name, Austin, which is a family name. Scott selected Levi's name, as he loves the story of Levi and his brother in the Old Testament where they protect their sister's virtue. It is a violent story, but Scott describes the biblical Levi as a "man's man" who did what a big brother should do. We named Levi for Scott by calling him Levi Scott. Finally, the name

---

19 Moore, Russell D. *Adopted for Life,* Crossway Books, Wheaton, IL, 2009, page 40.

Joel means "Yahweh is God."[20] A minor prophet of the Old Testament, Joel authored the Book of Joel. When we found out we were expecting, Scott was preaching a sermon series out of Joel and was inspired by several verses. We named him Joel Edward to honor Coach Eddie.

The girls, too, were to have a four-letter first name and were to be named after women who served Jesus wholeheartedly. The girls had an additional criteria: they would have double names—it's a southern belle thing!

We chose to name our biological daughter, *Katy Pierce*, named after Katherine Pierce, Scott's great aunt, with whom he had a close relationship; she was like a grandmother to him. He considered her to be the spiritual matriarch of his family.

Our adopted daughter would have a four-letter, double name as well: *Lyla Ruth*. The name *Ruth* represented my maternal grandmother, a wonderful example of a wife and mother who followed Jesus faithfully even when it was not easy. Also, I love the Bible story of Ruth; after all, that is the book of the Bible Scott chose to place my engagement ring in when he proposed.

Watching a movie one day, I first heard the name of *Lyla*; I really liked the way it sounded and how it looked when written. It even fit my four-letter first name pattern. However, I had never known anyone named *Lyla*, so it didn't fit my desire for her name to have a spiritual aspect. But, because I was stuck on that name, I decided to look up its meaning. In Persian, *Lyla* means "dark-haired beauty."[21] I thought that was appropriate, as she comes from a country where the women

---

20 "Behind the Name," *Behind the Name: The Etymology and History of First Names,* December 3, 2014, accessed July 6, 2015, http://www.behindthename.com/names/usage/biblical.

21 "Origin of the name Lyla," *babyname wizard,* 2014, accessed July 6, 2015, http://www.babynamewizard.com/baby-name/girl/lila.

adorn beautiful black hair. In Hebrew, *Lyla* means "you are mine."[22] This definition made my heart do back flips! The verse at the top of my blog and the one God laid on my heart about adoption is "I have called you by name, **you are mine**" (Is. 43:1b, ESV, emphasis mine). I knew this was the one; she would be *Lyla*. I sensed God was going to make her mine and His. Technically, she was already His; we just didn't know all of the details of how He was going to make her ours.

Our heavenly Father also knew Manjeet and Maduh's names; Scott and I found out about eight months later that "M and M" had been chosen by a precious family, the Watsons[23]. The Watson family is close friends to some of our friends in the adoption community in Columbus, Georgia; we have now become friends with them through our adoption support group online, and we would be able to get updates on M and M as they grew! It brought Scott and I so much joy and so much relief to know God had placed these girls in just the right home, and especially in a home that loved Jesus! And not only that, He arranged it so they would be adopted by a family that would become acquainted with us later and ease our troubled hearts that had been burdened for the girls for eight months. Coincidence? We don't think so.

---

22 "Female Hebrew Names and Meanings," *Fine Judiaca, 2011, accessed July 6, 2015,* http://finejudaica.com/pages/hebrew_names.htm.
23   Names changed for security purposes.

Chapter 7

INTERESTED?

MARCH 13, 2012 WAS A pretty spring day. After being trapped inside most of the winter, I was anxious to get outside and let the boys play. My good friend Janet Galyen came over to visit. I was a little over eight months along, and we were sitting out in the garage watching the boys play in the driveway. Janet and I were chatting like good friends do, when we were interrupted by a call from Scott. Calling from work, he told me Lori had sent us another referral, this time for only one little girl, but he had some concerns about this referral too.

Remembering the pain we experienced in turning down "M and M" in December, we decided it was best not to look at the pictures of any child in any referral to make it easier to stay emotionally detached. We had already let our adoption agent Lori know that, if at all possible, we did not want any pictures or files in the initial referral e-mails.

Thankfully, my friend Janet was there to watch the boys outside, because I was anxious to dash into the house, open up my e-mail, check things out, and try to figure out what Scott's concerns might be. I nervously opened my e-mail. The subject line read "Interested?"

I stopped for a minute, wondering, *is this the moment, the moment in which I will find out about my daughter?* I had been dreaming of the moment, and this could be it! My heart was pounding. I felt like I could not breathe. I opened her e-mail, and it said . . .

> Hi Scott and Kelly,
>
> I am not sure if you would be interested or not, but I have a gorgeous little girl born April 27, 2009 who has a hole in her heart and needs one surgery to repair it. Otherwise she is healthy and normal. She has normal growth, normal development . . . she is so cute.
>
> I was wondering if you would be interested in seeing her information.
>
> Hugs and blessings!
>
> Lori

I was ecstatic! Finally, a referral! I immediately called Scott so he could tell me his concerns, which I assumed were about her heart condition. He expressed he wasn't as concerned about her heart condition as he was about how we could manage to pay for a major heart procedure. Prior to notifying me, Scott had checked into our health insurance coverage and policies, and they said they would not cover her necessary heart surgery; it would be considered a pre-existing condition. He estimated this procedure would be about $50,000 if we paid out of pocket.

We both hung up feeling pretty discouraged. I was frustrated with Scott; it seemed like he had already thrown in the towel and this child would not be our daughter either. I, on the other hand, I am a fighter! I was not ready to give up! We agreed to discuss it further when he got home from work that evening.

The more I thought about it, the more the response from the insurance agent felt wrong. The recent Affordable Health Care Act had been signed into law and was slowly being implemented and integrated into most everyone's health insurance plans. One of its principles, stated over and over again in the news, was that health-care would be affordable for all families and all people. The Act also mentioned that pre-existing clauses would disappear. I wasn't sure why our health insurance could not help our family.

I was also concerned because our health insurance might cause difficulties with every referral we received. More than likely, each referral would be for a child with some sort of minor correctable special need that would require some type of surgery or medical attention. My frustration was just building and building.

Scott came home and I was bursting at the seams to discuss all of this with him. We had to wait until the boys were in bed so we could be more focused. Unfortunately, our discussion turned into a disagreement . . . Let's just go ahead and call it what it was, a fight! Scott felt I was pushing at a sad situation that was not going to change and that I shouldn't get emotionally invested in a child we were not going to be able to adopt. He was adamant we should not put our family in major financial debt. He had worked so hard to be a good steward of our many blessings, and he did not believe God would have us go into debt in order to adopt.

I argued, "This difficulty with insurance is going to happen with every referral we receive. There will be a 'concern' with every referral. When are you going to have enough faith to move past your concerns?"

I was being irrational and overly emotional. After all, I was eight months pregnant! I was not displaying the emotions of a godly wife as I was being stubborn and argumentative. And to be honest, he was right! I simply was not ready to give up on this girl. We said some things to each other and about each other that were not very kind that evening.

It wasn't one of our finest moments, but we serve a great God who had taught us a lot about forgiveness over the years. Scott and I were and still are committed to our marriage, which means we have to work hard at marriage in the good times and in the bad. Before we went to bed that night, we reconciled our differences and forgave the harsh words we said to each other, and we went to sleep after making this agreement: Scott would be willing to pray and seek discernment about this child for a few days, while I would take the few days to seek out as many options as possible to help this child get surgery. I promised Scott, if God slammed the door shut, then I would stop pestering him.

The next day Scott reached out to our local insurance agent to discuss the matter thoroughly and to make sure we understood our insurance policy clearly. We were wondering if they would even cover her generally, without the surgery, if she became our daughter. A door was slammed again, as the woman's response went like this: "By law, I have to cover your child, but we will raise your premiums to $2,000 a month."

I was downright angry and, to put it bluntly, ticked off. I felt wronged, like a disservice had been done to my family. Now I began to wonder if this was happening to families all over the United States. No wonder people had doubts and fears about adopting as the staggering number of orphans grew and grew!

I posted my rant on Facebook. I couldn't believe here was yet another situation I couldn't control—a needy child and no one to help her. I don't like the answer no, and I fight for what I think is right, so I immediately got on the phone to call anyone and everyone I could think of in the state of Tennessee to see what our rights were and what our child's rights would be.

To my dismay, I continued to run into dead ends. Talking with a clerk at the Tennessee Commissioner of Insurance Office, I was informed it was the local agent's right to raise premiums—that was how insurance companies were navigating around recent national and state laws originally drafted to protect adopted children. He explained, "In the past, some insurance companies refused to cover adopted children, but advocacy brought about laws stating they had to be covered. So in turn, insurance agencies raised premiums on families with adopted kids with pre-existing conditions to avoid high payouts for families."

This sounded so unfair. Scott tried to calm me by telling me insurance is a business and insurance companies are there to make money. This concept just bothered me to my core. When did it become okay to make money at the expense of needy children?

There were also a few human service agencies in Tennessee I contacted to help, but nothing was ever guaranteed. When we brought up the need for surgery, they would tell us that, even if they covered her, they would not be required to help with a $50,000 heart surgery.

I refused to accept a final "No." I contacted a lawyer in Nashville who put me in touch with some "higher ups" in some large insurance companies, in hopes they could help or provide me with more information. That's when Scott and I discovered that we were having this issue because of our particular policy. The way our family's insurance was set up was as an individual policy, not a group policy. According to the representatives I spoke with, if we had been covered under a group policy, the insurance would have covered our daughter and the surgery without question and without raising premiums. When my adoption agent said we were the first family with which she had experienced something like this, I was even more discouraged. The situation was looking grim. Doors were shutting left and right. However, there were some small glimpses of light, and I was willing to hold out to see if they could deliver any hope.

My new friend from Knoxville connected me to a heart doctor there who does a lot of mission work and is familiar with international adoption. This doctor gave us some hope that we might get this child a heart surgery in India for no cost, and then she would be completely healthy before she got here. However, he did mention there were several factors that would have to come into play for all of this to happen, and he told me to pray.

After two days of craziness and phone call after phone call, I took the doctor's advice and dove into prayer mode. I realized there was nothing else in my power or abilities I could do. I had to rely completely on God to take care of this situation. My prayer was if God didn't want us to have this child, God would need to completely slam these doors of hope. My prayers became more focused on the child than on our wants. Regardless of the situation, whether this precious little one could become ours or not, how awesome would it be if God could use us to help get this little girl healthy and secure her a surgery!

For the sake of our emotions, we reminded Lori we didn't want to view her full file as of yet. But I could picture a beautiful soon-to-be three year old, a child of God who deserved a healthy life and a loving family! I was committed to pray for her heart and seek help until God said to stop. "They will have no fear of bad news; their hearts are steadfast, trusting in the LORD" (Ps. 112:7, NIV). I clearly needed to stop and trust God to take care of our family and this little girl.

Over the next few days, we continued to hear from the doctor. He was the only one who was giving us good news; all the other doors had shut. This doctor was our one chance at helping this child and possibly being able to say "yes" to our referral. Scott and I decided, no matter what, we were committed to doing everything in our power to secure a heart surgery for this child, even if she could not become ours.

This doctor asked to review a copy of the little girl's agency file in order to send it to some surgeons to check into other possibilities. Scott and I had not seen any of her file information. Our agent sent the file electronically for us to forward and warned us there would be pictures in the file copies, and we should not open it if we were trying to protect our hearts from possible disappointment. We didn't open the file.

We sent the e-file copies to this doctor and to our pediatrician. A church member referred us to a pediatric doctor who was her relative practicing in Memphis, so we sent one to her as well. We were desperate for any input, answers, or advice these professionals could give us. Not only had we exhausted avenues seeking financial help for a potential surgery, but we were also now seeking medical opinions as to the severity of her heart condition, the extent of surgery it required, and the expectations for recovery. We were aware her file contained a full medical history, so these medical experts could inform us of any other medical issues we needed to know about.

The little girl's problem was an Atrial Septal Defect (ASD). According to the Mayo Clinic website, "an atrial septal defect is a hole in the wall between the two upper chambers of the heart (atria). The condition is present from birth (congenital). Small atrial septal defects may close on their own during infancy or early childhood."[24] In layman's terms, this sweet little one had a severe heart murmur too severe to repair itself on its own. Her murmur measured 14 millimeters and would require open heart surgery.

Knowing the pictures of this girl were on our computer presented a major temptation. I waited a couple of days and couldn't resist any longer. I sneaked upstairs to take a peek without telling Scott. I had one of those feelings again, right before I opened it. I wondered, would I be looking at my daughter? What was I going to see? Would I know for sure that this girl was the one?

I held my breath and opened the file; I would have to click on a link to see her picture. I paused and thought about it one more time. Was I sure I wanted to see her face? Oh, yes, yes, I did! I clicked . . . and there she was, this tiny little thing, dressed in pink, with a very sad, serious face. Yet

The first photo of Ami

24 "Atrial Septal Defect," *The Mayo Clinic*, accessed July 4, 2015, http://www.mayoclinic.org/diseases-conditions/atrial-septal-defect/basics/definition/con-20027034.

she was absolutely adorable and beautiful, and quickly I longed to make that sad little face smile. There was a second picture of her, a profile shot. When I saw her profile, I was amazed. I swear I thought she looked like us! She had the Parkison chin like my boys. She also reminded me of Levi and Seth when they look sad. I giggled out loud for a few seconds, thinking how God had carefully and specifically picked a child for us and how she would fit right in.

Since I had already sneaked a peek, I read her whole file. Her Indian name was *Ami,* and she had been in the orphanage since she was about nine months old. Another confirmation to me she was a match for our family was her birthdate of April 27th. This may seem silly but is not an exaggeration; most everyone in my family shares the same birthday, birth month, or at least the same numerical day of the month as another member of the family. For example, my grandmother and my youngest share the same birthdate of May 22nd, while my sister's is April 22nd. Scott's birthday is January 20th, and Seth's is May 20th. My Dad and his brother share the same birthday years apart. I was born on December 27th, and my mom, cousin, and nephew were all born on May 27th; how interesting that Ami's special day was April 27th! She fit right in date-wise. She had to be the one.

I could not stop staring at her picture. I closed my eyes and begged God to let her be mine. I wanted to make that sweet little face smile. I prayed Scott would feel the same. I slowly made the dreaded trip downstairs, afraid Scott would be upset I peeked at her without telling him. When I confessed to what I had done, he smiled and said, "I knew you wouldn't be able to resist!" He took off running upstairs to see for himself. I chased behind him. He saw her and quietly said, "Wow, she's adorable."

Chapter 8

BABYHEART

EVEN THOUGH WE HAD SEEN the face of this beautiful little girl named Ami, we delayed a decision to accept the referral or not until we could resolve our insurance issues and heart surgery decisions. A doctor from Knoxville was trying to help us, and it's essential I share the story behind it to point out how God works in all His awesome provision and glory!

Our church appointed a search committee to hire a youth minister. Their chosen candidate accepted, so he and his wife prepared to move to Manchester from Knoxville. I had met the new youth minister's wife, Rebecca (Becca), only during their interview weekend and over breakfast at Cracker Barrel. She seemed like a really sweet person, and I was anxious for her to get to Manchester. We had a lot in common. We would bond in friendship as we served our church family alongside our husbands.

Becca had started following our adoption blog after meeting me and chatting over lunch; she, too, has compassion for orphans and delighted in working in missions. She read my blog post where I had been in "panic-rant" mode about not having insurance or finances to cover our daughter's surgery. She was the very one who reached out to me to connect me with the doctor in Knoxville. She wanted permission to talk to the doctor about the child. Of course! I was thrilled to have help from anyone.

Becca attended church with Dr. Clint Dorion and had served at the orphanages Dr. Dorion started in Haiti and the one in the Dominican Republic called Chadasha. "The Chadasha Foundation is an international non-profit that provides spiritual and physical healing to the poorest of poor in Haiti and the Dominican Republic in the name of Jesus. The Foundation includes children's ministry, medical missions, biblical education, a heart program and support to churches and many other ministries in both countries."[25]

Becca shared my blog post with Dr. Dorion late in the evening on March 15; he responded the next morning:

Rebecca,

I am on the [Board of Directors] of International Children's Heart Foundation www.babyheart.org, and we operate on children free of charge who have congenital heart defects. We operate in two cities in India. Send me the child's echocardiogram and medical records and where the child is located in India. Does the child have a passport? No promises . . . this work will require prayer.

Clint

We hit our knees in prayer. I was overwhelmed with gratitude for my God and how He could make all of this possible through the kindness of strangers. I immediately reached out to Dr. Dorion after

25 "About," *Chadasha Foundation*, accessed July 4, 2015, http://chadasha.org/about/.

seeing his e-mail. He responded, saying there might be a medical team who could perform the surgery in the fall either in Hyderabad or Chennai. He kindly gave me a soft rebuke about my blog post that seemed to attack insurance agents. He was right. He did not need to say anything, because God had already convicted me about posting my anger. However, God made something good come out of it, since He used that very post to alert Becca to speak to Dr. Dorian.

God was moving, and we were doing our part to get all of the information to the correct people. This was when Lori sent the file with a warning that it contained photos. She wondered whether we'd be willing to adopt Ami if we were able to work out the surgery through the avenues we were pursuing. We wanted to shout "Yes!" but needed to wait for all the information we could before moving forward, and of course we needed confirmation from God before accepting the referral.

Dr. Dorion educated us about Ami's ASD and how it could be repaired; he even sent us videos of children with the same surgery so we could see their successful recoveries. It was through this e-mail we learned even more about the organizations Chadasha and Babyheart, and we were introduced to Dr. Novick, Medical Director and Founder of International Children's Heart Foundation.

Scott and I prayed earnestly for several weeks; Babyheart was scheduling their fall trip to India, and Ami could be receiving her surgery in October in Chennai. This was astonishing to us! Not just the fact we were closer to securing surgery for Ami, but we had close missionary friends who lived in Chennai: the Gupta family. They are the family who adopted the fifteen girls, the very place God spoke to me to adopt. It was blowing my mind how God was piecing all of this together.

Scott, naturally, was still concerned with all the unknowns involved. It was yet another situation testing our faith and resolve. There were so many tiny details involved in planning the surgery, and here we were on the other side of the world, doing our best to make everything work out.

I continue to be amazed with the way God intervened and used a blog post to get us to this point; His plans and designs are matchless! He was working out miracles and, unknown to Ami, she would be the benefactor. God was allowing us to be a part of His handiwork; I was awestruck when He swung a door wide open for her when other doors had slammed.

During Seth and Levi's spring break in late March, we decided to take the boys to the Nashville Zoo. I was only a few days from delivering Katy Pierce, and we decided this would be our last big hurrah before we became a family of five. It was late in the afternoon, and we were winding down our visit to the zoo when Scott received a call from Dr. Dorion. Scott talked with him a little while. Dr. Dorion even placed another doctor on the phone who had performed this particular surgical procedure hundreds of times and, coincidentally, there was a good chance this particular doctor might be the one doing Ami's procedure in India. While Scott spoke with them, the boys and I sat on a bench and watched the elephants while I rested my very pregnant self.

Scott came over and took my hand. We prayed together as a family. Scott said he was somewhat hesitant because there were still so many unknowns, but Dr. Dorion had been very reassuring. Scott felt

God's consent was apparent, considering all He had worked out thus far. We officially should accept the referral. My heart was filled with joy! I think I could have done laps around the zoo at that point, even being 39-weeks pregnant with swollen ankles!

We waited through the weekend to pray over our decision, and we contacted Lori on April 2nd to let her know we would officially accept the referral. We were anxious to do the additional paperwork and learn what was involved in moving forward. A couple of days later, on April 4, 2012, Katy Pierce Parkison was born. It just felt like the perfect little trifecta, the birth of our daughter, accepting the referral of our daughter in India, and securing her heart surgery (for free, I might add)!

April was an exciting month for us. Huge milestones were happening in our family, and we felt incredibly blessed. We ended the month celebrating our Indian daughter's third birthday on April 27th, even though she was not with us. It was a small family affair, but seated in the kitchen and looking into the eyes of my husband and my three precious children, knowing we had another daughter who should be there before the year was over . . . it felt complete.

I still longed for her, wishing she could be there to eat the cake Seth helped me make for her. I could see her big, sad black eyes looking back at me through her picture. I was ready for her to come home.

Once we secured our daughter's heart surgery and our referral, I felt like our process should be on a roll. The waiting we did from the end of December until mid-March had been our difficult waiting period everyone in the adoption circles talks about. And trust me, those few months of waiting on a referral were pretty tough, especially having completed all of our paperwork and having turned in all of the money. So our wait was almost over . . . right?

I do not know if I was naïve, blissfully unaware, or living in straight up denial, but I had decided our daughter would be here no later than Christmas. I boldly informed family and friends we would have our Lyla by Christmas! But I was wrong . . . we were headed into a nightmare!

This nightmare to come would reveal my strengths and weaknesses as a person, a Christian, and a parent. Moms often speak of the hardships of pregnancy and childbirth, saying, "The pregnancy and birth were difficult, but once the baby came, I forgot all about the hard stuff." I certainly could relate to that sentiment with my biological children. Waiting for this daughter, I would be facing "hard stuff" too, but this time with no child in sight.

The next year and a half of our adoption experience is not one I would wish on anyone. I know it happens to many families not only in the United States but in other countries as well. Unlike moms who can forget the hard stuff of pregnancy once their baby is born, I will never forget the horrors of waiting on my Ami/Lyla's arrival.

Chapter 9

WAITING

THE BIGGER NIGHTMARE BEGAN WITH one of the things I hate the most—waiting! Once we accepted our referral, we did not hear much from our agency. I had expected a weekly run-down of the progress of our paperwork and how it was moving along on the Indian government's side of things.

On our side of the world, we had to submit more paperwork. We needed to re-apply for our I-800 approval to adopt. We had written and applied for adopting a child with minor correctable special needs, but due to her heart condition, Ami was considered a child having major special needs. So, we re-submitted our paperwork to USCIS, which delayed our approval a few more months. It took us a full day to fill out our new paperwork and submit it, but then it would go through all the proper legal channels, which would take some time. We were seeing firsthand why our home study caseworker advises families to broaden their parameters on their home study paperwork. We had changed ours to include more children, but we hadn't changed our statement to include more severe special needs at the time.

Once again, we went for a few weeks with no word from our agency. I reached out to Lori in mid-May, looking for hope, information, answers, a timeline—anything! I wanted to find out if our daughter knew a family in America had accepted her and ask if we could send her any items. Our agent replied that our daughter would not know about us until after the No Objection Certificate (NOC) was granted. Until our I-800 approval came back, nothing else could move forward. She advised us not to send any packages to the orphanage because those items rarely end up in the hands of the kids. That statement made me cringe and my stomach hurt. How could someone rob children of care packages from their families? Especially someone who was caring for my precious child?

Lori also encouraged me to redirect my focus from worrying about our approval to working out the plans for our daughter's surgery and where her caretakers would be staying during her surgery and recovery. Lori must have picked up on the fact I do not like to wait; giving me something to do in the waiting period was an excellent idea.

However, Scott decided we should wait (there's that word again) until we had our official I-800 approval before we started making arrangements and plans for the surgery. It was not until early July that we received our approval from USCIS, which was good to have, though the wait set us back about three months.

With the approval in hand, we contacted Babyheart to make arrangements for our daughter's surgery and for her caretakers. But again, we were told to wait. A representative from Babyheart cautioned us to wait to make any plans regarding the surgery until mid-September, because sometimes their trip dates were changed or even cancelled due to various circumstances.

August brought us a glimpse of hope and some new beginnings for me personally. On August 1, we received a confirmation e-mail from the United States Embassy in India stating they had received our provisionally updated I-800 form; the next step in our process would be to fill out a *DS230 Part 1* and *Part 2* form and send it along with a photograph of our daughter. The photograph arrived in an e-mail from our agent soon after. Here was my glimpse of hope. At this point, I had seen only my referral pictures of my daughter.

It's hard for me to describe this picture. In some ways, she looked absolutely precious; in other ways, it bore a resemblance to someone from a concentration camp. Her head was shaved, and she looked frightened. It gave me a sense of urgency to get her home as quickly as possible! My family and friends, especially Seth and Levi, wanted to know why her head had been shaved. Because of my mission trip experiences and working with orphans, I knew orphanages tend to keep children's hair short to prevent lice infestation. However, I still thought she looked beautiful. I don't know many girls with a shaved head that can carry that look off quite as well as our cute little one!

It was during this month of August that Scott and I had discovered we were expecting once again, another new adventure our family would embark on but one we were familiar with. We were shocked when we first found out! Even though I always wanted a large family, I went into panic mode, worried how we could provide for all five children after all. Plus, we just had Katy Pierce and were adopting a child. As anxiety took over, I called our moms and my close friend Leslie from church to be sounding boards and an encouragement for me. Of course, their first reactions were to laugh (I think they were in shock too) and then say "Congratulations!" Yet, nothing brought me peace and assurance like my husband. As I sat crumpled over in tears on the couch, Scott came over and placed his hand on my stomach; he prayed and thanked God for the incredible blessing of a new baby. He was right! God would take care of this new baby, just as He had been watching over our adopted daughter.

God had been so faithful, and our friends and family and even strangers had been so generous in giving towards our adoption expenses. God raised every penny needed for our actual adoption. However, with the surgery coming up, we would need to raise more money to cover the extra costs for flights, food, and hotel stays for our daughter and her caretakers during her surgery and recovery. There would most likely be costs for medications. The surgery would be taken care of financially, but we were unsure of what the hospital would charge us for her care, so we wanted to make sure we were prepared for any possibility. We guesstimated that we would need about $2,500 for these extra costs.

In addition to being a pregnant mother of three children, serving as a pastor's wife, and performing other duties required of me, a new opportunity had presented itself where I could earn some money without being away from my kids. I started doing direct sales and selling Scentsy Fragrance products.[26] Direct sales was an unusual fundraising strategy, but I felt God was leading me to do this in order to raise the needed funds.

I was first introduced to Scentsy products through my Mom. She bought me a couple of warmers as gifts and some Scentsy buddies for my kids. Shortly after I received these gifts, everyone who visited my house commented on how great my house smelled. After being asked

---

26 Website: www.kellyparkison.scentsy.us.

how to order Scentsy products over and over again, and after much prayer, I decided to sell it myself, and I started off on my new adventure!

I am still in awe when I think about the way I became involved with Scentsy. Ten years prior to this time, I held the title of *Miss South Carolina 2002*. Then, after my involvement with the reality show *The Amazing Race* in 2004, I was asked by about 25 companies to sell various products, everything from skin care items to kitchen items to home decorations, all of which I respectfully declined. For the first time in ten years, I said yes to doing direct sales and, to be quite honest, I wasn't asked; I felt led to it. I sought out Scentsy to sell their products.

I was nervous at first, worried I wouldn't be successful, but due to a great product that sells itself and the motivation behind my desire to make sales, it was well worth my efforts. Somehow the fact I was working a job in order to donate my profits toward our expenses made me even more confident and determined. Because of this successful venture, God proved He was facilitating our fundraising efforts again—through Scentsy!

Other financial support came from friends in our church. Many families worked diligently to collect donations on our behalf. Again, it was a reminder that God is with us and He cares!

On August 16th, we got another ray of hope that things were progressing well. We received our Article 5 Letter from the United States Embassy in India. I blogged:

> *Because your love is better than life, my lips will glorify You. I will praise you as long as I live; and in your name I will lift up my hands* (Ps. 63: 3–4, NIV).

I tell you that there is nothing like starting your day out with a quiet time, a quick work out, a shower, and an e-mail from the United States Embassy in India! This morning I heard the most formal yet beautiful words I have heard in a while, as Scott read aloud . . .

"The United States hereby grants legal custody of Ami to Scott and Kelly Parkison."

Finally, things seemed to be moving and moving quickly. Only two weeks had passed since we sent in the DS230 form. Now we heard our paperwork was being sent to CARA in India. Other than the judge who officially grants custody of adopted children to families, CARA is pretty much the "end all" for adoptions. Very rarely will a judge deny a family custody after CARA approval. But at CARA, families wait for the NOC to be issued, which is one of the largest final steps in the process. My agent told me that once you have the NOC, there is pretty much nothing to stop the adoption from happening.

A few days later, we received our third set of pictures. It was a fantastic, unexpected surprise. Our little girl was dressed so pretty

in a white dress, and she was even posed on a toy car and in a chair. She still had the same scared face with no hint of a smile, but she looked adorable. I longed to wrap my arms around her even more.

August continued to look up! I found out the Southern Baptist Convention, which is our denomination, gave a small grant to pastors' families who were

Ami on the toy car

adopting. We received that grant to help us with our additional expenses with the upcoming surgery.

Things were going smoothly, it seemed, but at the end of August we hit a bump in the road. I blogged:

> *She is clothed with strength and dignity; she can laugh at the days to come* (Prov. 31:25, NIV).

I am clinging to this verse right now, and trying to remember that with faith I can laugh at the future. In other words, I am not going to worry. I am not going to fear. I am not going to get down. I am not going to hit the panic button. I am going to trust in my Heavenly Father who has led us this far and provided answers and provisions all along the journey of adoption. So here it is . . .

We got word today that Babyheart, the organization that was going to do our daughter's surgery in India, has now cancelled their trip to India.

What does this mean for our girl? She is okay healthwise for now, but will need this surgery in the coming years. What does this mean for us? Well, I guess right now we aren't sure. We are looking into many options. She has to have the surgery in India for insurance purposes here in the States, but we know God will take care of this! It also means that we will be fundraising even more, since we may have lost this opportunity at a free surgery. But I am up for the task!

What does this mean for you? This means we need your prayers. Pray for God to once again provide for our need. To find a place, a doctor, and to provide the funds needed.

Thanks friends! Your prayers are priceless to us!

Many of our friends, burdened for us, sent us links to organizations and companies that might help us financially with her surgery. Even Mayor Mary Hawkins of Madison, Mississippi, my mother-in-law's hometown, heard our story and tried to secure a potential surgery for us in Jackson.

However, Dr. Novick with Babyheart and Dr. Dorion came to the rescue. They committed to helping us secure a doctor and a hospital and even negotiated a price as well as personally helped with some of the funding of her surgery. While there were some uncertainties about the specifics of it all, we felt like God and the generosity of Dr. Dorion and those at Babyheart were going to get us through this little bump!

By early September, Dr. Novick had secured for us an experienced doctor in India and negotiated the costs, and Dr. Dorion was helping us with the funding. They even went as far as to secure a date in October to perform the surgery. I was doing the happy dance! Everything was working out!

Then three days later, we received an e-mail from our agent saying the orphanage didn't have any caretakers who could take our daughter to get her surgery. AHHHHHHH! Our friends at Babyheart had spent so much effort in securing a surgery. How could the orphanage back out on their word, and *now* of all times? This was one of the first things we made sure of before we officially accepted the referral, before we even secured Babyheart. The orphanage had committed to getting Ami there if we paid for it. My happy dance was beginning to look more like a tantrum.

Our agent suggested two new options. We could try to locate a hospital and doctor within Ahmedabad, the city where the orphanage is located, or we could wait to have her procedure done after the adoption was completed and stay in India longer when we picked her up. The second option is what we originally thought was going to happen. The only catch with that option was that it could require us to be in India for up to five weeks. That would require a lot of timing and planning, especially since we had three, potentially four other kiddos who would need 24/7 supervision.

We prayed and studied both options. Babyheart did not have any contacts in Ahmedabad. Dr. Gopi, a doctor in Hyderabad who was originally supposed to do her surgery, said he would be willing to do her surgery anytime and whenever her adoption was completed. So it appeared we would be spending a good amount of time in India when it was time to pick her up.

On a side but equally important note: a woman in our church, Nancy Walker, told me she would travel with me to India for the child's surgery and recovery, if Scott couldn't stay the whole time. That gave us a little more security in the second option as well.

In the midst of all of this back and forth with the surgery, we continued fundraising with Scentsy. I had started an additional fundraiser with the help of two friends in church. One of our deacons at the time, Dennis Flatt, and our church pianist, Janet Layne, got together and recorded a CD of music for me to sell to raise funds. It was another way God was showing He was in control and that the adoption was going to happen, just not the way I originally planned it, which is ultimately the best and better way!

Things seemed to be moving forward. The additional funding was coming in and, according to our agent, we should have our NOC anytime. Well, October rolled around and still no word of the NOC.

My heart dropped when our agent informed us she had received word that a particular woman within CARA was delaying our NOC from going through.

That was a zinger to hear. Why would someone purposefully delay paperwork to prevent a family from coming together? My agent had no answers at the time, but I was certain forces of darkness were at work to resist, subside, and push away anything that could bring God glory.

So many reasons ran through my head regarding why this lady halted our NOC. Having been to India before, I knew orphans are considered "untouchables," which means there is little value placed upon their lives. Why would this lady care if little Ami received a loving home? Did she hate Americans? Did she have a problem with Scott being a pastor? My mind was racing.

On Halloween, we received more pictures of our sweet girl and the news that CARA agreed to issue our NOC. Yes! We trick-or-treated that night with extra pep in our step. Scott and I were estimating a timeline and felt we might be traveling to get her around January or February.

Mid-November came, still no NOC and no new information. Each passing day with no word turned my thoughts into insanity. I was trying really hard to hold myself together emotionally and spiritually. I wanted to appear full of faith, but the questions started to come and played over and over in my head.

By the end of November, my agent sent an e-mail stating our case had now been approved by SARA, which is the state government agency for adoptions, and it had been sent back to CARA for final approval. She felt this would be completed before Christmas.

In mid-December, we received an e-mail from Lori stating our case was in court. This e-mail didn't mention our NOC, which was supposed to come first, but I did not care. I was elated when I read the e-mail. I quickly started recalculating when we'd have the chance to meet our daughter.

Even though I daydreamed about our travels to get her, my heart felt something was wrong. We tried to contact Lori for about a week with no response, which was not like her. She was very reliable and always responded within a day or two. I was thinking this would be a time she would be rejoicing with us because going through court was the final phase.

While waiting, I began to burn with anger; why had she not e-mailed or called? Finally, an e-mail came. I read it in anticipation, but to my disappointment, it was a brief e-mail explaining she was off for Christmas break. I told Scott I could not sit through two weeks without answers.

Christmas Eve, Scott called her and left a terse voicemail, stating we expected a call. She e-mailed her response, a Christmas Eve bomb that she didn't want to send and we didn't want to receive. Lori had learned our case had not passed CARA but was instead placed in a special committee for review before being approved for the NOC.

At the time, we did not know what a special committee meant, but it sounded scary. It seemed like we were being robbed of more precious time with our daughter. And on top of that, there were no explanations or details to help us understand.

We celebrated Christmas and held onto each other a little tighter that holiday season, reminded that family is a gift and could be taken away at any moment. On January 8th, we finally got the clarification we had been looking for. I blogged:

> We desperately covet your prayers over our adoption for the next couple of weeks. In my last post, I shared how there had been some miscommunication in our adoption process, and we were told it is in a special committee for review. At the time we really did not know what that meant.
>
> We finally got some clarity yesterday. It turns out our case was sent to CARA in September. (CARA is an Indian Organization that approves all adoptions and is the 2nd to last step before an adoption is complete. In addition, when they grant the NOC, your adoption is pretty much official. The child is yours. Then the NOC is followed by court dates that get all the paperwork in order, and then you go receive your child.)
>
> The woman who received our case . . . . gulp . . . denied us. She stated our biological children were too young. According to our agency, which has handled many adoptions from India, and according to Indian Adoption Laws, my family meets all the criteria to adopt the little girl we were matched with last Feb 2012. Apparently this same caseworker has been denying other families as well, for no real good reason.
>
> Because my family meets all the requirements within the laws, our case was filed again, to be granted the adoption of our little girl. Since this is the second time through, it has gone to a special committee.
>
> We have been told that this committee will meet within the next two weeks. Our agency asked us to write letters about why we want this particular child so much. Needless to say, it was rather emotional for us. Even the

grandparents wrote letters, and Seth drew a picture of him and his sister playing.

How do you put into words how much you love a child you have never met? Because our family truly does love this child like she is already here. We have a room for her, clothes for her, toys for her, Christmas presents waiting on her bed from her grandparents . . . we already feel she is a member of our family. We love her like our biological children . . . already.

I asked our agent if we could lose her, and I appreciate her honesty. She said we do have reason to be concerned. One positive thing she said is that there is someone within the CARA organization that is advocating for us. So we are asking you to pray and be advocates for us too!

Scott says he has a complete peace and is not worried. He feels it is all going to work out. Me, on the other hand, my faith is shaky right now. All I know to do is pray for God to work on the hearts of the committee, so they see how our family is where our little girl should be placed.

I know He is in control . . . sometimes it is easier for me to say that than put it into practice. Please pray for me too!

Our recommendation letters consisted of phrases like "for the sake of Ami, the sake of our two sons, and for our sakes, we are writing to beg you for your approval of granting our family the *NOC;*" "In our hearts and minds, she was immediately a part of our family, our extended family, and our community;" "I fear if we do not receive the *NOC,* it would be like a death in the family. My wife and I would feel we had lost a child;" "Please let us continue with this so as not to delay this surgery for Ami any longer than necessary;" "Please, we beg this of you! Please let us bring our daughter, Ami, home;" "Please be aware that Scott, Kelly, and their children will not be alone in this adoption. They have our undying committed support as grandparents who are here, ready and willing to spoil little Ami with all the love we can;" "We are saddened to tears to even fear the heartache that would happen in all of us, but mostly we worry about breaking the hearts of our two grandsons, Seth and Levi, who have waited for Ami patiently and with arms and hearts wide open, ready to be Big Brothers to her;" and "They have a natural gift of relating to children at their own level, and are never condescending. Our grandchildren love this about their parents, and we can't wait to have a new addition to this loving family." Along with the letters, Seth drew the most precious picture of himself and his sister playing outside with the words written in his 5-year-old handwriting, "I love Sister Ami." This picture still hangs on my refrigerator today.

Two weeks came and left, and our agent said it could be another month before the special committee met. I was very apprehensive that this was going to drag on and on and on. The last time our case was in CARA, which was September, it dragged on for three months until we learned that it was in special committee. I was struggling with trusting God's will, especially because I had no control over the outcome or the process. It was in others' hands but ultimately God's hands. Scott was a rock. He never wavered and stayed strong, full of joy, and full of faith.

When February rolled around with no word of any movement in our case, I hit rock bottom emotionally. It was difficult for me to talk or blog about. With every word written, I felt completely drained. I was trying hard to be upbeat and full of faith but could no longer carry out the façade. Every word I would type was a reminder of all the time I had missed spending with her that day, and even scarier, I might not ever get to spend time with her.

I finally blogged:

> I am not really a negative person, in fact people tell me I can find positive in most situations. But this was one tough journey, now getting close to a two-year journey. I don't regret one second of it because I have grown personally in this process. Here is the dreadful part of this experience . . . Me. There were times when I was so down, impatient, doubtful, hopeless, angry, and frustrated, but the beautiful part of this experience is displayed in how God was bringing me through it and developing my character, how He provided through all of it, and how she is almost home. I guess the only thing I hate is that every day is one more day without her here. But I am consoled by the fact that God is in control and can make anything good out of anything bad.

In addition to blogging, I placed a strong effort into developing a prayer group on Facebook and meditating on Scripture.

The LORD will fight for you; you need only to be still (Ex. 14:14, NIV).

> Consider it pure joy, my brothers and sisters, whenever you face trials of many kinds, because you know that the testing of your faith produces perseverance. Let perseverance finish its work so that you may be mature and complete, not lacking anything. If any of you lacks wisdom, you should ask God, who gives generously to all without finding fault, and it will be given to you. But when you ask, you must believe and not doubt, because the one who doubts is like a wave of the sea, blown and tossed by the wind. That person should not expect to receive anything from the Lord.

Such a person is double-minded and unstable in all they do (James 1:2–8, NIV).

Blessed is she who has believed that the Lord would fulfill his promises to her! (Luke 1:45, NIV).

Just in time for Valentine's Day, we received precious pictures of our daughter in a white dress. I could not get over her tiny feet. I felt she might think she moved to the land of giants when she finally joined us! We also learned there would be a national adoption conference in India on the 19th and 20th, and the special committee stated they would be meeting about our case after the conference was completed. I went ahead and prepared my heart; this did not mean they were going to run out the door and meet right away. There was a good chance we were still many weeks away from a meeting.

Once again, February came and left with no word from the special committee. My faith, husband, and prayers of other believers carried me through this time. I had already been to rock bottom, but people were sustaining me with their prayers and encouraging words.

Other little pockets of blessings along the way helped me cope. An Indian family had moved to our town, and when we met them, we learned the husband was from Ahmedabad, and they spoke Gujarati. They had a sweet little girl close in age to our Lyla. They invited our family to their daughter's birthday party. It gave me hope and reminded me that one day we would be celebrating our daughter's birthday as well. Incredibly, God was providing us with a family who could help communicate with our daughter if needed, since they spoke her language!

One morning after a Mom's Bible study, I was at McDonald's with several of the other moms and their children when I received a call from my agent. Though she was a little reluctant to give this anxious mama hope because there were no guarantees, she told me her contact at CARA had said our case would most likely be resolved in our favor in the near future. This particular advocate was waiting for the right moment to get our case through. I wanted to jump for joy, but she quickly reminded me, "Stay grounded and continue to pray, because nothing is final until they grant us that NOC." CARA still could deny us the adoption of our little girl and insist we pick another child. They could still delay the time to make their decision. Nothing was final, but it was good to hear something positive!

When she ended our conversation by saying, "I suggest you focus on the children you have right now," a lightning bolt of rage shot through me; I was far along in my pregnancy, and the stress and anxiety of waiting just added to my irritability. In the agent's defense, I know she meant no harm; she was trying to comfort this crazy mom on the other end of the phone who had been nagging her for answers week after week after week. But even though I knew she didn't mean it the way I took it, I was still frustrated.

First of all, I love all my children. Our life never stopped through this crazy, lingering, long intermission. We still went to work, played in the park, went to prenatal appointments, worshipped, played ball, celebrated holidays, and traveled. Simply put, I *was* focused on my children. It just so happened that one of them was in an orphanage in India, and I was focused on her too. Even though I did not have a piece of paper in my hand stating she was my child, she was my child in my heart. I love all of my children deeply and fiercely.

The agent could tell the conversation was taking a turn for the worse; she comforted me with Scripture and quickly rang off.

I think every family, no matter what agency they use, has moments of frustration with each other. I have met only one family that has adopted internationally from South Korea, and they experienced a smooth process lasting only six months. Most families I have spoken with, especially those from India, have all had some sort of hiccup in the process that made the partnership of the family/agency relationship difficult to navigate.

Being an agent is surely a rewarding yet exhausting position. Each family yearns for their children and wants their process to go as fast as possible. I am sure there are lots of parents (including me) who ask for updates often in the process, looking for any indication that their process is almost over. Yet, in my opinion, an agent cannot communicate too much. Better to over-communicate than not to communicate at all!

Okay, climbing off my soapbox now. We had some hope, and I was willing to go with it! A week later a representative from our agency went to CARA in New Delhi to work on resolving our case. Soon we heard they would be having the final deposition about our case; we should know in one week if the NOC would be granted. There was something powerful about the word *final* to me in that e-mail.

The word *final* was exciting, as it indicated this waiting game was coming to an end and I would soon embrace my new daughter, but it was also scary, because the outcome might not be in our favor. Then the Lord gave me these Scriptures:

> *Who of you by worrying can add a single hour to your life?*
> *Since you cannot do this very little thing, why do you worry about*
> *the rest?* (Luke 12:25–26, NIV).

Rejoice always, pray without ceasing, give thanks in all circum-
stances; for this is the will of God in Christ Jesus for you
(1 Thess. 5:16–18, ESV).

Encouragement also came from another "Indian Momma"—as we call ourselves—Kelley Parmar, through my Facebook support group. She was in the adoption process and a client of my agency. We discovered we had other similarities: many similar spiritual God moments in our adoption, both she and I and our daughters share the same name but spell them both differently. Kelley sent me an encouraging message with this Scripture that allowed me to rest and wait on what seemed like the week that lasted forever:

> I will go before you and will level the mountains; I will
> break down gates of bronze and cut through bars of iron. I
> will give you hidden treasures, riches stored in secret places,
> so that you may know that I am the LORD, the God of Israel,
> who summons you by name (Isaiah 45:2–3, NIV).

Our agent told us we should know if we had approval of the NOC by Friday, April 5th. We held a prayer meeting at our house the Tuesday before. About ten people from church were there to pray with us and for our daughter. Other friends who lived much farther away wrote and let us know they were hosting their own prayer meetings on our behalf.

We received an e-mail the next day in which our agent confirmed the final deposition would occur April 5th. Thank goodness I had a lot to keep me busy that week! I was planning Katy Pierce's first birthday party, and I was going to the ob/gyn more as I neared the end of my fourth pregnancy.

Finally it was the eve of April 5th, and I remembered an experience I had on my first mission trip to India. We had spent nearly the whole trip in various orphanages all over the country. The final orphanage we visited hosted about 300 kids, which was way over their occupancy limit. Still, the orphanage would not turn anyone away, and for that I am glad. The orphanage had a special program for their foreign visitors, and each age group of children sang and performed for us. I'll never forget these young girls who appeared to be 12-13. They sang a very familiar hymn in English, "Because He Lives."

I had sung that old hymn since I was a little girl, but never had it had an impact on my life until I heard these sweet girls sing it. Sure, they were singing along with an out-of-tune guitar, and I could certainly hear their accents. But, when they sang the words, *"Because He lives, I can face tomorrow. Because He lives all fear is gone. Because I know He holds the future, and life is worth the living just because He lives."* The meaning of the lyrics became real to me. Those girls standing among the hundreds of seated orphans knew the true meaning of those words. They had lost their families, they slept on a hard concrete floor each night, they shared small portions of food so everyone could eat, and they had experienced real fear. But they knew life was worth living anyway because Jesus LIVES! I could never sing that hymn in the same way again.

It was on that very trip, as a single woman, that God laid the desire to adopt a little girl from India on my heart, and here we were almost eight years later. The next day was a big day of results for my family and our adoption. But guess what—*Because He lives, I can face tomorrow. Because He lives all fear is gone. Because I know He holds the future and life is worth the living just because He lives!* I was ready for Friday! Although my agent had said we would more than likely not know the official answer until Monday, I knew tomorrow was the big day!

On Friday evening, we celebrated Katy Pierce's first birthday with a small ballerina party at my church. My mom came to town to celebrate with us. After the party, we came home. Mom bathed the kids, and Scott left to run some errands. I thought I would take a quick peek at the e-mail . . . just in case.

Indeed, an e-mail from Lori was there, and the subject line said, "YES!!!!!" Her e-mail read, "Yes! The special committee has approved formally for Ami, and by next week the committee officially will send a notification to the NOC committee for issuing the NOC. This may take a couple of weeks. We are hoping by the end of this month the NOC may be granted and this is my guess. But it's on the move, phase by phase."

I went into a quiet shock. All of the waiting was finally over. She was officially ours. I prayed to God, thanking Him for what He had done. I sat there at my dirty, sticky kitchen table with tears streaming down my cheeks. I called Scott because I simply could not wait until he got home to tell him; he was so happy and relieved. I ran to the bathroom where my boys were splashing in the tub and told Mom the great news. She responded with shouts of excitement!

We had just celebrated the birthday of one daughter and now had the official approval of our other daughter on the same day. What an amazing day! Scott walked in the door, and we greeted each other with a kiss and a huge bear hug. The long waiting phase in our process was finally over; although we knew we had some more waiting ahead, we could handle the rest of the proceedings with great expectation of what was to come. Speaking of great expectations, soon our little Joel was born. This new baby comforted me as I waited for the NOC.

The official NOC arrived on June 18. The next step was going to court to be approved by a judge of the high court in Gujarat. They usually go to court for three or more sessions, and it can take three months or longer.

We were deep in our summer activities, busy with visiting family, beach trips, Vacation Bible School, sports camps, and church camp. On the way home from visiting family this particular summer, we extended our trip and stopped in Columbus, Georgia, to meet five of the families from our Facebook adoption support group. All of us used or were using the same adoption agency. One of the families had recently returned home from India with their daughter, and it helped to hear about their recent experience.

It was a special time to connect with these other moms in person. One friend was my high school classmate who helped us select our agency. Another friend, Amanda Carroll, and I had grown to be very close via the Internet, due to her children and my child living at the same orphanage. She was as anxious as I was to get her son and daughter home. Knowing our children would have a connection to each other in the years to come brought us joy.

Our family spent the night with the Carrolls; we went to church and had a delicious Indian lunch before we headed back home. I learned during our get-together that I might be able to find our court case and where it was in the process through the Gujarat High Court website. I researched online the next few days for our case.

Score! I found it. To officially see our family's name on the docket was great, and not only that, but to see that our first case was happening that day, August 2nd, praise God! I continued to check the site daily to see when our next hearing would be and found it was happening on August 26th.

Soon we learned our final court hearing would be on September 7th. I suddenly went into nesting mode. My little girl could be here in the next couple of months! I was ready to get the house in order like I did for my other babies. I was in total planning mode. Every day, I checked prices online for flights and planned where my four other babies would go while we were away. I was thinking about lice removal kits and learning how to use them if needed. I gathered what I thought a four-year-old might need during our time in India.

Additionally, I created two books online to give to our sweet girl. One was a book with a poem I wrote to her. The poem is entitled "Forever." I planned to read it to her daily for a long time so that she would one day grasp the meaning of the word and the significance of it in her life. I pray she will always know that she is now a part of our family forever and that she will be forever loved.

FOREVER

Forever is a long time
it never has an end.
It lasts for always
and again and again.

You will come to know this word
engrave it on your heart.
Forever will never leave you
it will be there from the start.

Forever will never hurt you
or ever bring you pain.
Forever will walk with you
through sunshine and rain.

Forever is not here to fix you
or your story of the past.
Forever wants to grow with you
in a story that will last.

Forever wants you to know
there is nothing you can do
you can be mad, sad, or even bad
Forever will always love you.

Forever wants to sing and dance with you
and tuck you in at night.
We will say prayers together
and know everything is alright.

Forever comes in different forms
it can mean time, commitment, and fate.
I found my first forever
when I was only eight.
I learned of a man
that came to seek and save the lost
He had bought me at a price
He said I was worth the cost.

I can't wait to tell you all about Him,
and read together the best story of all time.
Because I am forever His
and He is forever mine.

My second forever came
a little later in my life.
He promised to always love me
and he took me as his wife.

You will know this man as Daddy.
He makes every day shine.
And I am forever his,
and he is forever mine.

Then came more forevers
in the shape of little ones . . .
Seth, Levi, Katy Pierce, and Joel.
With them there is always fun!

These are your brothers and sister.
You will come from the same line.
I am forever theirs,
And they are forever mine.
And then there is you
My new forever
We will walk hand in hand
In this journey together.

I will forever love you
with a love that is divine.
Because I am forever your Mommy
and you are forever mine.

The second book was a picture book; I hoped to use this book to help with communication. It had pictures of our family, our house, and also pictures that would help us talk to her while in India: pictures such as planes, cars, forks, bath tubs, and toilets. These would be things she had never seen and never used, but once we arrived she would be on a plane several times, riding in cars several times, and learning to use the other items.

Most traditional or "Pure Indians," as they are sometimes called because they have not conformed to the Western world, eat with their hands. Scott and I love to eat with our hands when we are in India. However, we knew our new daughter would have to use utensils here in the United States, and we would need to start working with her on those skills. In addition, we would probably have to train her to use a western toilet, as most Indians use the squatty potty.

We had also learned that there was a strong chance we were going to need to travel before our daughter's passport was completed. In the normal process, a family would not travel until the child's passport and travel visa were completed and in the hands of the orphanage. However, with our daughter's surgery and her recovery time, we could be pushing the limit of thirty days with her travel visa.

This, of course, was great news; perhaps we would get to see her even earlier! But my agent said it was not definite. We would have to wait until the court proceedings were finished.

With all of this in mind, it appeared we could possibly be leaving mid-September, and I would stay for about four to five weeks, while Scott would stay for two. The hardest part for me about this plan was being away from my other children, but God had already been bringing me comfort about this. And, I thanked Him for the Internet, because I would be able to FaceTime with them every day!

Something else nagged at me as the process dragged on. I became more concerned about renaming our daughter. In adoption circles, it is a highly debated and emotionally charged topic. I was struggling with the thought that she was four now, and that would be like someone telling my four-year-old son, Levi, that his name would be changed. I prayed for God's clarity about it and decided I would know once I met her.

Well, there wasn't much time to nest or worry. According to the Gujarat Court website, the final court date was set for Saturday, September 7th. I anxiously awaited news of its completion in order to make travel plans. We found out that Monday, September 9th was a holiday in India, and the courts were closed. Therefore, it was safe to assume we wouldn't see an update online until Tuesday or later, but I still looked every thirty minutes. Yes, I confess to checking for updates constantly for several days in a row. Even then, at the end of the adoption process, my character was still being shaped by God in the area of patience.

After picking Levi up from pre-school on Tuesday afternoon, I had to run home to meet someone. I normally didn't come home after getting Levi because I waited to pick up Seth too. Nevertheless, once at home I took a quick look online, and there it was . . . the word *Disposed*. Our case had been disposed; that's how it is listed on their court reports when the cases are closed.

Immediately, I let out some sort of shrill exclamation, and then I clapped violently while jumping up and down. Then I realized I needed to call Scott, but I could not find my cell phone (surprise!). I frantically ran/skipped through the house and squealed at the same time and finally found my phone. I turned around to find Levi looking at me like I had lost my mind. With a very concerned look on his face, he asked, "Mommy, what are you doing?" To which I replied, "It is finished, the court case is finished! Lyla Ruth is going to come home soon!"

Next, I broke down and cried and finally called Scott. After that, I went through a roller coaster of emotions again, screaming with joy, laughing hysterically, crying tears of joy, and then repeating the cycle a few more times. I am sure to the average person I would have looked very strange that afternoon. After I told my friend Amanda Carroll that I was a hot mess of emotions, she said, "Well, you deserve it!" I agreed, so I continued on my emotional roller coaster for at least two more hours.

Scott came home, and we met at the back door and embraced tightly. I cried a little more in his arms, as I could not believe it was finally over. Scott said, "I feel like you just gave birth." And he explained he felt the same euphoric feeling he had when all of our other children were born.

Scott has said that I, as the mother, have a physical and emotional attachment with our kids from the moment I find out we are pregnant, and he does not really feel that deep bond until the day the children are born. But, that afternoon, he finally had that same connection, the one I had been feeling all along. His daughter was ready and waiting on us to come get her. It was a very sweet time of rejoicing for us both. The long wait was finally over!

Chapter 10

GOTCHA!

EVEN THOUGH OUR CASE WAS disposed, we waited until the orphanage received the paperwork from the courts before we made our travel plans. Another tangle in the planning would be matching our travel plans with the doctor's availability. He had some vacation time pre-planned, and we needed to work around his schedule as well.

Once again we found ourselves waiting, but this time more patiently. If by a miracle the paperwork arrived in the hands of the lawyer or the orphanage in the next few days, we could be leaving the next week. However, if it took more than a few days, we would be forced to wait until October due to the doctor's availability.

Waiting, waiting, waiting, waiting . . .

Early Monday morning, September 16th, our paperwork arrived and we were cleared to pick up our daughter. We could leave as early as Wednesday the 18th, just two days later. Along with this news, our agent told us the lawyer for the orphanage expected an additional $500 for expediting our paperwork from the courts to the orphanage. What a downer in the midst of the excitement; we had no room in our budget for this unexpected expense. I questioned the legitimacy of this request for extra payment. Perhaps someone used bribery and passed the expense to us to expedite our paperwork, or maybe they were taking advantage of foreigners and our helplessness in the circumstances. We didn't have time to worry. We decided to pay what we could without going into debt and trust God!

Now, the only thing hindering us from booking our flights was confirming the dates with the surgeon. Around midnight of Tuesday morning the 17th, the e-mail came through. Our daughter was confirmed for surgery in Hyderabad!

We couldn't sleep for excitement and spent the next few hours working on booking flights. We sent an e-mail to Adoption Airfare at 3:00 A.M. and were totally surprised someone called us back at a little after 6:00 A.M. during non-working hours. What good fortune to be on the phone early in the morning with an agent! She answered our questions and worked hard to secure flights for us during her non-working hours!

We would take off the next day, Wednesday the 18th. This is how the Parkisons roll! We planned a five-week international trip in 24 hours! These are the things we did from early Tuesday to early Wednesday morning before we left:

Scott and I woke up at 6:00 A.M. after three hours of sleep. We hurriedly dressed Seth and Levi for school and fed breakfast to Joel and Katy Pierce. (The older boys would eat at school.) Scott drove them to school and went to his office to arrange and reschedule his church matters. He contacted all of our credit card companies, asking them not to automatically freeze any unusual spending coming through from India. He also collected all major documents and made necessary copies. He took the car to have the oil changed for traveling to the Atlanta airport.

Back at the house, I was washing all our dirty laundry and calling all the major players—who had agreed to help with the kids—to inform them it was time! I e-mailed our itinerary and contact information to each caregiver. I cancelled doctor appointments for the next two months and rescheduled meetings I had planned. I handed off the entire Women's Ministry Retreat duties and went over the schedule of the retreat with another friend. (Thanks, Robin!) I telephoned and recruited some volunteers for another church function. I made a few *Scentsy* sales and placed the order for delivery to my customers, and then I did laundry, laundry, and more laundry! After packing for four kids to go different places, I finally started packing my own bags before hurrying off to the notary for important papers and the store for shoes to fit tiny feet. I picked up a few toiletry items and essentials for the trip and snagged fast food for dinner. (I think we ate it!) My hair and feet were attended to at 9:30 P.M. thanks to my hairdresser's willingness to work after hours. (Thanks, Jessica! You're a true friend.) Finally, I finished packing, charged the electronics, and cleaned the house the best I could. WHEW! I thanked God for all He had set in place and for all He continuously provided for us this busy day in so many ways.

First and foremost, God gifted Scott and me with the most amazing feeling of peace in the midst of all of the chaos. We were neither stressed nor anxious as we completed our tasks and chores, and we were quite joyful anticipating what tomorrow had in store for our family.

After I posted our news on our blog and the word spread among our church family and friends, God nudged and prodded our friends to reach out to us. Our friend Peggy called and offered to watch the kids all day Tuesday! (Thanks, Peggy! What a big help!) She would come to watch them at our home so I would not have to be away from them this last day. While I concentrated on completing our tasks, she played with them, fed them lunch and dinner, and prepared them for bed. It allowed me the freedom to do the things I needed to do. Without her help, I don't think we would have been able to make the trip, or at least no one would have had clean clothes!

God provided last-minute availability for the twenty different caregivers who would supervise our kids while we were gone. Because of the love these caregivers have always demonstrated for our children, we could breathe a sigh of relief, knowing they were going to be taken care of and, in fact, most likely spoiled! These twenty caregivers were made up of family members and church friends who would watch our four children over a four-week period. The Deuermeyer family even offered to meet my parents halfway to South Carolina to deliver Seth and Levi to them. All of our caregivers and friends would continue to help Scott with the supervision of our children when he returned from India a few weeks ahead of me. What a blessing to have family and friends who are obedient to God's urgings and sacrifice for no reward.

Other friends encouraged us with texts, phone calls, and e-mails that declared their joy for us. Several church friends dropped by the house, ran in, hugged us, and some people dropped in to leave gifts for us to take to our daughter. In addition, throughout the day, four separate people came by and said God had laid it on their heart to bring us money for our trip. I remain astounded! Their financial gifts more than covered the amount we needed to pay that unexpected additional expense of $500, and we would have a little extra for "just in case."

His provisions continued to pour in. The Carrolls, our new friends in Columbus, Georgia, saw our post on Facebook and offered to store our car for free at Amanda's parents' home in Atlanta while we were out of the country. It would be safe there and save us the cost of long-term airport parking. Amanda drove from Columbus to meet us in Atlanta and drive us to the airport; she and Jeff were only a few months behind us in the process of getting their son and daughter from the same orphanage as our daughter.

At the airport, we joyfully cried and hugged and said good-bye, knowing Amanda fully comprehended our anticipation and joy, and realizing our adopted children were most likely together at that same moment. I told her I could not wait for it to be her turn. I was determined, even if it was not procedural, to do everything in my power to meet her kids while I was there getting Lyla Ruth, and I would do my best to deliver some gifts to them and take pictures for her and Jeff.

Waiting to board, Scott was like a little child filled with excitement. He was beaming and laughing and plain giddy about going to meet his daughter. We carried on our tradition of eating a bacon cheeseburger in the airport before departing to a country where beef and cattle are sacred.

However, God still was not finished! Living in India was an adoptive couple we "met" on Facebook, and when they read we would have a layover in Mumbai, they sent a message. These two new friends picked us up at the airport, displaying a cute welcome sign, and drove us to enjoy a Starbucks coffee during our four-hour layover. We sipped our favorite coffee, ate delicious pie, and enjoyed great conversation. Our friends had recently adopted from Ethiopia and gave us some new and helpful advice about what to expect. Most importantly, they brought us an Indian cell phone so we could contact them if we needed anything! They told us to keep the phone and to pass it on to someone else who may need it when we were leaving.

What thoughtful acts displayed by our many Christian brothers and sisters; if they had chosen not to call, message, or offer their help, we would have never been the wiser, as it was not Scott and I who asked for these favors. We were, and still are, so humbled and blessed by all of our family and friends' generosity and the kindnesses we received from strangers who are now our friends. And most of all, we stand in awe of the incredible God that we serve!

We did not arrive in Ahmedabad until 2:50 A.M. Friday, the day we would be getting our daughter. By the time we arrived at the hotel, unpacked, and took a shower, it was 5:00 A.M. I tried to sleep; maybe I did a little here and there, but not much. We had a wakeup call set for 8:00 A.M., but that was unnecessary since I was up and ready to roll at 7:00 A.M.

I have a tradition for the day I give birth to my children; I do my best to look as beautiful as possible. As if competing in a pageant again, I apply full make up and style my hair. Scott has always poked fun of my little ritual; he even has a video of me in mid-contraction asking for lipstick. I do this because I want to look my best the first time my child meets me, and I felt the same about meeting the newest member of our family.

I had selected an Indian outfit to wear, a pink silk one given to me by a former church member in North Carolina. I loved that it was pink; it would represent a new daughter. I put on full make up and fixed my hair in a pretty bun since Indian women usually wear their hair back, and I wanted to look as Indian as possible for my girl to feel comfortable when she met me for the first time.

I chose to wear a costume jewelry pearl necklace because of a dream I had a few days prior to leaving for India. In my dream, I took off a necklace I was wearing and placed it around our daughter's neck when I met her. So, before we left for the trip, I bought this pearl necklace to wear and to give to her. It would be a keepsake just for her.

Before we departed, I glanced around our hotel room to make sure everything was in order. The couch and table in the corner of the room were filled with colorful packages and gifts from grandparents, church friends, and her brothers and sister. I couldn't wait to give them to her and show her how much she is already loved.

Scott and I headed down to eat breakfast and wait for our taxi to take us to the orphanage. I think I might have eaten about three full plates because my mind was on overload. I was a little nervous about the big day that lay ahead, asking myself all kinds of questions: What is she going to be like? What will she think of us? What is her personality like? How will her transition into our family go? How will we communicate? Will I get to see my friends' children too? We were about an hour away from knowing some of those answers.

Our taxi arrived. I carried a bag of supplies that consisted of items other Indian mommas recommended for making that first meeting a little easier. I was loaded up with gifts for Ajay and Smita from the Carroll family, and I carried my iPad and a camera charged and ready for video and snapshots.

The taxi ride felt surreal, like a dream. I interviewed Scott during the ride to record his thoughts. He spoke to Lyla: "Honey, one day you will see this. I just want to let you know we are on our way to get you. We feel so blessed you are going to become a part of our family. We are so excited, and we love you very much."

When we arrived at the orphanage (what Indians call an *Ashram*, a place for destitute people), it was not at all what I had pictured in my mind. In my previous experiences in serving in orphanages in India, they were all stand-alone buildings with acres of property surrounding the building. I could not even distinguish our building from others. It was smackdab in the middle of all sorts of other buildings squeezed side by side on a busy street. Even our taxi driver was unsure which door we were to enter. He asked around and soon led us to a door with an iron gate in front of it. We rang a buzzer, and a woman opened the door dressed in a sari. She looked surprised to see us there. Didn't they know we were coming today?

The woman did not speak English, but our taxi driver verified we were in the right spot and told us to go in. Some agencies provide advocates or representatives to be with families during this step, but this was not a service provided by our agency. Thankfully, we had been to India before, so being a minority and unable to communicate was not a stressor for us; we had grown accustomed to it on previous trips.

We walked straight into a room similar to a small, open lobby. A long desk sat on the right side of the room, which was lined with a few chairs. The only light at that moment was the sunlight coming in through some windows and an open corridor past the long desk leading to some sort of courtyard. In the courtyard, I could make out some plant life and greenery and a little bit of another building, but that was about all I could see. Everything looked very clean, simple, and sterile. There were no decorations or anything sitting on the desk. A clock and a picture of a man, who I assumed was the founder, were the only items on the wall.

Another woman met us at the desk and motioned for us to sit down. She did not speak English either, so we all sat there in silence for about twenty minutes. Of course, my nervousness and excitement were growing, and I began fidgeting like crazy. I gave Scott a rundown of pictures we should have taken when we finally met our little girl. It was the only thing I could think of to talk about.

A young Indian man entered and informed us that Mr. Pandit, the overseer of the orphanage, would be there very soon. Ten minutes later, he arrived in the form of an older man with a very pleasant disposition.

We spent the next forty-five minutes trying to understand each other and communicate questions and answers regarding the procedures to obtain our daughter's passport. Our difficulties at communicating made me start to feel tense. Scott and I were under the assumption our daughter's passport would be there when we arrived to claim her. We needed and expected to have it before we left for her surgery. We gleaned from Mr. Pandit's mix of broken English and Gujarati that we could go ahead and take her to Hyderabad for the surgery, and the Ashram would mail her passport to us when it arrived. But we certainly did not want to book flights to Hyderabad if we needed her passport to fly. If we didn't have the passport, what documentation would she need in order to board with us? All of this took us by surprise; we weren't prepared for it and figured they would add an extra charge for providing the documents that weren't there.

We ended up phoning our agent Lori and another agent to make sure we were all on the same page. While Scott was on the phone, he walked over to the door that led back out to the street. I stood with him, listening in on his conversation. We were shoulder to shoulder, but while he faced the street, I faced the lobby.

And then BOOM, just like that, I saw my girl. In an instant, she walked in through the corridor, quite unsteadily I might add. I had been warned by the other adoptive moms not to expect my child to be able to walk stably yet. She actually reminded me of Katy Pierce, my 17-month-old toddler at home, the way she was staggering along just to move forward a few feet as her caretaker led her our way.

Her entrance surprised me. I guess I had pictured this big pro-duction in my head of our first meeting . . . cue the Miss America theme song, "There She Is," add the confetti and fanfare, and she would make her grand entrance. Yet, it was quiet and simple; I just turned, and there she was. She was very tiny and appeared extremely confused and so very serious.

I could not believe it! She was actually standing there in front of me, looking exactly like her pictures. She was dressed in a cute turquoise outfit with hideous black shoes on her feet. Her hair was very short, and she still displayed the same solemn expression we had seen in all of the pictures. She carried a clean, cute stuffed animal. She refused to look our way and stared off to the side.

I could not move; I think I was in shock. Again, nothing was going the way I had planned. Scott, still on the phone, was not even aware our daughter was standing close by. Unsure whether or not to wait for him to get off the phone before approaching her, I couldn't take it any longer, I went to her. I walked over and knelt down, trying my best to get to her eye level so perhaps she would look at me. It was simply impossible to get on her level because she was so tiny, but at least I was closer to her now. Even though I had moved within reach, she kept averting her eyes away from me, afraid to make eye contact.

I could tell she was unsure of what was happening. I could see the scared and confused expressions on her face. Her caretaker held her hand and spoke to her, trying to make her look at me and give me a hug and kiss. She would glance at me and then quickly look the other way. I was okay with her just looking at me occasionally; I wanted her to feel comfortable first. The caretaker slowly backed away into the corridor, peeking around the corner to watch us interact. I kept motioning for Scott because he was still on the phone. At last, he realized she was there.

He ended the call, grabbed the camera, and knelt down beside me. Scott reached out to gently touch her face and sweetly told her, "I know you don't know who we are yet, and this is all very strange to you. But I am your Daddy, and this is your Mommy." It was a very precious moment and reminded me of how Scott held each one of our biological children in his arms after their births and introduced himself, speaking softly and tenderly to them. My eyes welled up with tears; this moment would join the other cherished memories of Scott meeting our children for the first time and would remain in my heart forever.

Meeting Lyla for the first time

We were finally meeting *Lyla Ruth* for the first time! I called out to her using her Indian name, Ami, although once we left the orphanage with her, we would begin calling her Lyla. I said *Ami* to her several times in hopes of getting her attention. She still ignored me! Suddenly, I remembered my dream and the pearl necklace. As I went to take it off my neck, she glanced at me and this time began to watch me remove it. It took me a few seconds because it got caught in my bun, so that bought me some more eye contact time with her. She was still looking at me as I placed it around her neck, and then a few seconds later she turned her head away again. Now Mr. Pandit approached and tried to force her to kiss Scott. She refused, and I was proud of her! I was glad she was bold enough not to feel like she had to do anything. I knew she would show affection in good time.

Scott meeting Lyla for the first time

Mr. Pandit then proceeded to give me the run down on her: what she eats, when she eats, when she sleeps, and how she does with using the bathroom. The caretaker was still there, standing in the corridor, and I could tell the child was more secure with her there. One time the caretaker walked out of her visibility, and when she returned, it was the first time I saw Lyla give a slight smile. It comforted me to know she felt connected to someone there. It also gave me hope that one day she would connect with us. Soon the caretaker left the room for the final time.

We began to ask about Jeff and Amanda's children who lived there, Ajay and Smita. We wanted to see them and take pictures for the Carrolls. Mr. Pandit escorted us through the open corridor and into a small room on the left. This room had one small desk and chairs around the outer rim of the walls. We still did not walk as far as the courtyard, but from what I could see, the courtyard was huge and open with several lush plants and trees. If I had to guess, it compared to the size of a high school gymnasium. It was hard to believe all this was on the other side of the little iron-gated door we entered at the beginning.

When we settled in the tiny room, Mr. Pandit offered to bring us some chai and cookies, which we gladly accepted. He told us Ajay and Smita were on their way. While sitting in the little room, we gave our Lyla a sucker. She was not sure what to do with it; she just held it in her hand and would not let it go, even to unwrap it. I sang songs and tried to play with her, but she just sat there and looked the other way. However, she seemed interested in Scott. She watched everything he was doing. The longer we were with her, the more comfortable she grew with us, and I was relieved to see her relax a little bit.

Finally, we broke the ice with the use of the iPad. I showed her a picture of herself on the screen, and she managed a little grin. It was a funny grin, one where she tried not to grin, so we couldn't see her actually smiling. But it made her look even cuter, because her lips puckered out when she did it.

Soon Ajay and Smita arrived. Ajay walked right up to Lyla and patted her cheek, and she smiled at him. It brought me joy to see they knew each other, because we would definitely see them again in the future. They had beautiful smiles and entertained us with a song. They were so precious, and I was honored we got to hand deliver gifts from their parents and sisters. I could see they were going to fit right in with the Carroll family.

After they left, our chai and cookies arrived. Scott signed papers with Mr. Pandit as I played with our daughter and tried my best to break through her tough exterior and get her to smile. I got one!

Mr. Pandit, the lawyer, Lyla, Scott, and I

Finally, we walked out into the beautiful courtyard to take some pictures. I saw they had a banana tree on site, and Mr. Pandit pointed out some other things about the surrounding building that I could not grasp. It appeared there were bedrooms surrounding the whole courtyard, almost like a hotel. There were a few children across the way, but it was too far away to really see any faces.

Dreading it and unhappy about being forced to part with precious money for questionable expenses, Scott went to make the exchange of the money to cover the $500 additional costs our agent said the lawyer added on at the last minute. Scott considered refusing to pay or trying to negotiate but feared it might lead to interference with the adoption. Therefore, trying to be a good steward and at the same time trying not to jeopardize the adoption, he decided to hand Mr. Pandit only $200 to see how he would respond, hoping he would accept a lesser amount. Mr. Pandit accepted the lesser amount, shook Scott's hand, and gave him a hug. Scott saved us $300.

Mr. Pandit seemed to enjoy our company. He was adamant we not leave until we met Mr. Patel, the attorney. Mr. Patel was an older gentleman; when he arrived, we took several pictures with both of them and with their cameras too.

Since we had not slept much the last several days, I was rapidly becoming physically and emotionally exhausted. I was more than ready to get in the car and head to the hotel and have our little girl to ourselves. Based on the information passed on from other Indian moms, I knew this day possibly would get longer and more difficult. How would my new daughter react to leaving the only home she had known to go off with light-skinned strangers?

I had done my best at researching bonding with a child. I read books, listened to podcasts, and talked with families who had gone before us. But every child is different and will respond and react differently to their new life and new family. Knowing that, I tried not to have any expectations and to see what transpired.

Before we left, Mr. Pandit handed over a huge file with all of Lyla's records. We said our good-byes and again made sure we could leave without her passport, assured they would mail it to us. On the ride to the hotel, following the advice of other moms, I was prepared with a plastic bag to catch her vomit in case she was car sick; after all, it was likely she had never ridden in a car. However, she didn't need it. She just looked around and tried to take it all in. I am sure she was still trying to figure out what in the world was going on.

Taking more advice, I was prepared to do something I had never done before when we arrived at the hotel—and I was quite nervous about this—delousing her. Thankfully, she appeared not to have any lice or nits. But just in case, I decided it was best I still treat her and comb through her hair. We started off with a shower for her. I showed her the water for a while and let her reach in to touch it. We had a tub, but I felt the shower would be best. The shower had one of those removable showerheads with a hose attached so I could control the water. She seemed very comfortable with the shower and the water. She even grinned while I was running the water over her.

Next we wrapped her up in a clean towel, sat her on the bathroom counter, and began the delousing process. She is definitely a McCorkle (my maiden name) at heart. She loved having her head rubbed and massaged. She grinned while I rubbed the delousing foam in her hair. I even gave her a little Mohawk hair-do in honor of her brother Levi, who likes to spike his hair up too. I put some lotion all over her, and

Painting Lyla's nails

she seemed to enjoy being pampered—definitely signs of a girly-girl in the making!

Then, we dolled her up in a new outfit and opened her gifts. She immediately went to the nail polish, so I painted her little nails pink for her. She must have had her nails painted before because she knew exactly what to do. She held her tiny hand out and kept her hands really still after they were painted.

After her nails dried, she looked at a hand-sewn photo book my friend Andrea made, in which I inserted pictures of our family for her. She loved touching the pictures and holding the book. I spoke the names of her brothers and sister as she touched photos of them. I also spoke her name, Lyla Ruth. I wanted her to learn to recognize it as her new name.

Next, she played with her first Barbie. She was more interested in the tiara that Barbie was wearing and pretty much carried the tiara around with her the rest of the day. I was pretty sure I was in the presence of a future Miss America. We played for a couple of hours and then snacked on some cookies. I think she was worn out because she begged to crawl in the bed.

Our playtime together allowed me to observe several things about her. First, I saw she was beginning to smile; actually, they were more like sideways grins as she was trying not to smile. It was so cute. I observed that although she was four years old, her skills and abilities appeared much younger. She displayed similar capabilities to my 17-month-old at home. For example, I sat her on the couch in our hotel room to play with her dolls and walked away for a second. She fell off the sofa and bumped her head. We then realized she had probably never sat on a sofa before or possibly even a chair.

When she bumped her head, she cried. It was a good bonding moment for us to let her cry in my arms. I wondered while holding her if she had ever been held before when she cried.

I noticed her tiny frame, and how again, she was so similar to Katy Pierce, my 17-month-old. Lyla, could easily wear 18-month size clothing at the age of four. She was (and still is) my tiny, petite princess! I wondered if her small size was due to her heart condition and a lack of nutrition in her diet.

Periodically throughout the day, she would sit cross-legged on the floor and rock back and forth. This was her coping mechanism. She would usually start whimpering and crying. Any time I saw her get in that position, it alerted me she was about to have a breakdown. Sometimes I could get through to her and distract her before the tears came, but if she got worked up, I would just hold her. I knew she was trying to figure out what was going on, and she probably missed her routine and all the things familiar to her. I felt honored and blessed, even though it was hard to watch her hurt emotionally, to be the one to hold her as she cried and to try to comfort her.

Little did I know those little moments of grief were building up to the worst episode yet. We went to a restaurant for dinner. As soon as we sat down, Lyla began to weep and cry very hard. We decided to head back upstairs and eat later. Once we returned to our room, she wanted out of my arms. I went to try to comfort her, but she pushed her hand out to indicate she did not want me. She did the same to Scott. She began to take her bracelet off that he had given her. She took her flower headband off. She would not take a new toy or the doll we had given her.

She walked (staggeringly) over to the window and pointed out. She said something we could not understand; I assume it was in her native Gujarati language. This was the first time we heard her say anything in a different language. But she got her point across; clearly she was calling for someone else. It almost sounded like *Momma*, but it wasn't. I'm not sure what the word was in the midst of her bawling, but I bet she was calling out for her caregiver.

She sobbed uncontrollably. She even began to try to take her dress off. She was making it very clear, without speaking English, that she was saying, "I don't want you or your stuff. I want to go back to everything I know."

This did not hurt our feelings. It only hurt to watch her hurt. We got down on the floor as close as she would let us and watched her sob. We wanted her to know we were right there, and it was okay. She could come to us if she needed.

Trying to be positive, I was thankful she felt the freedom to show her emotions. Other moms said sometimes children are taught not to act scared or cry or show emotions, because the parents who had come for them would be mad or disappointed. This was not the case with little Lyla; she had no problem showing her emotions to us! We watched her uncontrollable sobbing for thirty minutes non-stop.

We waited patiently, sang songs to her, and prayed for her. At one point, I got on Facebook and asked our church to pray for her. Immediately people wrote back saying they were praying. Well, the prayers worked! After about a good 5-10 minutes more of hardcore sobbing, Scott reached for her, and she went to him. He took her on a little walk around the hotel.

After they left the room, I completely lost it. I had a breakdown of my own and a moment of guilt. *What have I done to her,* I thought. *Did I do the wrong thing?* I cried out to God in prayer, and He brought me comfort and brought to my mind a beautiful picture of His love for me and my own adoption to Him. Adoption is such an excellent picture of God's love for us. It demonstrates His loving pursuit of us and His desire to rescue us from abandonment.

We are nothing like God, even though an adoptive parent symbolically plays a similar role in pursuing, rescuing, and loving a child. Scott and I played that role in this story of Lyla's adoption. But on the contrary, this whole adoption process has shown me how completely opposite I am of God! I have been extremely impatient, angry, doubtful, faithless, scared, whiny, rude, grumbly, and even emotionally unstable. I mean, at times I acted like a little kid who didn't get her way.

And then there it was, the reminder God sent me. I felt as if He were telling me, "Your little girl is like you, Kelly. I want you, and I have made Myself available to you. I sit close by even when you don't want Me there. I continue to reach for you even when you deny Me. I love you regardless of the fits or tantrums you throw. I long for you to be in My arms. I want to carry you and walk with you and show you wonderful things."

That picture in my mind and the words that were coming through to me—Pure Peace. I was reminded of God's call on my life to adopt a child, and I was assured we did do the right thing.

Scott and Lyla returned to the room shortly. She was still a little weepy, the kind of weepy when, after having cried so hard, it's difficult to breathe without gasping every now and then. She kept doing that hard breathing thing for a few minutes; I reached for her, and she came to me. We picked out a lollipop together, and she selected a chocolate cookie and became calm. She sat in our arms and enjoyed her snacks. A chocolate cookie always helps things, doesn't it? Soon she started grinning with us again. She initiated play with us, and we saw some teeth smiles for the first time. It was joy to this Momma's heart!

We played for a while and ordered room service since we missed dinner altogether. Then we started the bedtime preparations. I worried bedtime might trigger more grief, but I was wrong. I learned being sleepy makes her silly and giddy. She was giggling and laughing. When we tried to brush her teeth, she laughed hysterically. She thought it was the funniest thing! It was the kind of laugh that was contagious, and soon all three of us were laughing hysterically.

She slept through the night and slept hard, and when she awoke, she did not appear sad. One thing I was not concerned about was that this girl was covered in prayer; she had been prayed up! I was certain our friends and family near and far were praying for her, as we were, and it was working.

Our first full day together on Saturday went great! She woke up in a very pleasant mood, and we started off brushing her teeth again, which she still thought was so funny! We went down and had ourselves a delicious breakfast at the hotel.

Speaking of breakfast, the girl could put some food away! She always wanted to snack on goodies in the hotel room, and then she ate about two plates of food when we sat down for meals. She was eating mostly fruit, roti, and rice. We ventured out and gave her some chicken for the first time. We were pretty positive she had never eaten meat. Survey says: Winner Winner Chicken Dinner! She liked meat.

She had this methodical way of eating. She was very careful, sat up straight, and ate very slowly. Actually, there was one meal where she was so excited to be using a fork by herself that she kept stuffing her mouth and laughing, but the rest of her meals she ate slowly. She was careful not to spill one drop of water, her drink of choice. If a small crumb fell into her lap, she would pick it up and eat it. We also noticed she would cram as much food as she could into her hands while snacking and sometimes while eating. In the orphanage, she must have learned if you put food down, you lose it. Therefore, she grabbed as much as possible because she had never had much. She hardly ever made a mess because she didn't want anything to go to waste. I hoped she would rub off on my other kiddos when it came to not making a mess!

She had another meltdown after breakfast that morning, but this time it was different. Instead of pushing us away, she came to me and wanted me to hold her. This was a big step in the right direction. We were earning her trust. She cried for a good twenty minutes. We finally found something to distract her from her sadness: the television. She watched about thirty minutes until she fell asleep.

After a good long nap for all three of us, we headed into town to find our baby some brand new shoes. I had brought several pairs of shoes with us from the States in different sizes, but her feet were so tiny, none of them fit. Lyla was already struggling with her mobility, but when she wore the ugly black shoes from the orphanage, her walking was even worse.

We bought her a pair of tiny black sandals. It was the only pair in the store in her size. She was so proud of her new shoes. In fact, when we got back to the hotel, bathed, and got ready for bed, she wanted to wear her new sandals with her pajamas. She colored and played while I packed up to leave for Hyderabad the next day.

We could see more progression in our bonding. I could tell she wanted to be near me; she followed me all around the hotel room as I was packing. I could

Scott and Lyla bonding

also see she was bonding more with Scott, and I got the feeling more and more that she was going to be a Daddy's girl.

Chapter 11

OPERATION

ON SUNDAY MORNING, WE WOKE up early to fly to Hyderabad. We got our little one up at 4:15 A.M. However, I knew what to do when she first got up to brighten her day: brush her teeth!

Scott and I prayed really hard for Lyla Ruth the night before, as this would be another day of hard transitions for her. It would be her first time on an airplane, and we were leaving the hotel, the only place she had been besides the orphanage. There was finality to it; we were leaving the only home she knew.

She surprised us; this girl was tough as nails. She did not shed one tear that day, on a day I expected breakdowns. She did great at the airport and on the plane. She thought all of the little bumps of turbulence were funny, and she loved receiving the free airplane snacks!

In the airports, several groups of Indian women were fascinated with us because we looked like a unique family. I spoke the phrase "Goad Liya" (*adopted* in Hindi); my friend in Mumbai said it translates "from one lap to another." When I told people she was adopted, they became excited. They chatted away in Hindi, and I knew they were talking about us because they stared at us as they talked. Most always though, one person would stop and look at Lyla and touch her face and say she was blessed.

We arrived in Hyderabad, which seemed more tropical with its beautiful greenery and palm trees. Lyla enjoyed being toted around in the airport luggage carts by her daddy. Of course, Scott was driving her around as if she was in a racecar, like he would with our other kids. She loved it and kept wanting more!

That second day we spent with Lyla, we began to see more of her personality and were amazed at how much she was like our other kids. On the first day we met her, we actually thought this would be the one child in our family who sits still and is very quiet. Ha! What were we thinking? That was just first day jitters! She was very active, silly, mischievous, and talkative. She was non-stop chatting away in her Gujarati language. We had no clue what she was saying, but she just kept on and on.

During the first few days with Lyla, Scott and I laughingly quoted Mr. Pandit over and over again: "She is not funny." When we picked her up from the orphanage, she had a serious, somber look on her face and would hardly crack a smile. The director of the orphanage told us at least three times, "She is not funny." Now, we could hardly get her to stop laughing, squealing, playing, and playing practical jokes.

Her mischievous side really showed during the car ride from the airport to our new hotel in Hyderabad. A gigantic Indian version of a wasp flew into our car. Scott and I jumped and started leaning forward to get away from the bug. Lyla burst into laughter! She thought it was hysterical we were scared of the bug. She waited a few seconds and then tapped Scott and pointed to the air to indicate the bug was right beside him. He jumped and swatted again, but there was no bug. She had tricked him. She laughed the hardest I had yet seen. She was quite full of herself that afternoon.

This was another day when I recalled sound advice from one of my Indian Momma friends, this time from Gwen Lewis. Once we arrived at the hotel, I could feel major exhaustion setting in, and I could tell Scott and Lyla were getting tired too. Gwen had mentioned the major exhaustion she had experienced in the beginning of the bonding process. She talked about being physically and emotionally spent because she had to pour into her child 24/7 to help the child connect with the new family. I was living that exhaustion she referred to now; I had been pouring everything I had into Lyla.

I was all about observing Lyla when I was awake, and with the time difference across the world, I knew my other kiddos were asleep. But then, when it was our bedtime, all I could think about was our kids at home, because I knew they were up and awake. I kept reminding myself that God's love and protection stretches around the whole world, and even though I was far away, He was with them. With the time difference, all the emotional experiences, and the massive travel we had done, we all crashed. The next day was going to be a big day for us. None of us knew what to expect on hospital day.

Monday, we woke early and enjoyed a delicious Indian breakfast in the hotel. It was a large breakfast buffet, and all the various foods were labeled. Scott came back to the table with a huge plate and told me I should taste this chicken he had because it was so moist. I took one bite and knew I was not eating chicken meat. I asked what the label said from where he selected it. He went over and read it. "Chicken lever," he said with a shrug. I burst into laughter. It was a misspelling of *chicken liver*. We laughed and laughed, and even though Lyla had no clue, she laughed with us!

We were a little nervous about heading to the hospital to meet with Dr. Gopi for Lyla's evaluation. We expected to walk there, but Dr. Gopi arranged a car for us. The hospital was not very far from where we stayed, maybe a five-minute walk. The hospital was a tall building jam-packed India-style between other buildings. Our driver quickly escorted us into the hospital. The initial lobby we walked into was packed with people, just like any emergency waiting room. However, we were the only white people in the room, and we were carrying a beautiful Indian girl. It felt as if we were movie stars coming through, the way everyone was staring and the way we were being madly escorted through all kinds of doors to get to Dr. Gopi's office. Scott said he felt like royalty.

The last door opened, and I recognized Dr. Gopi from his picture online. He was a very nice, well-spoken man, very interested in why we wanted to adopt and why we chose India. We chatted a bit more and talked about possibly getting together for dinner while in Hyderabad. He explained our visit was only for an evaluation. They would admit her on Tuesday—the following day.

Dr. Gopi then sent us to Dr. Suman, another wonderful doctor, to get an echocardiogram. It was at this point we learned Dr. Gopi would not be doing Lyla's surgery or procedure; instead, Dr. Suman would be. When we met him,

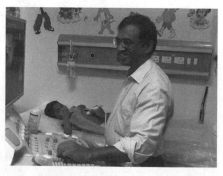

Dr. Suman looking at Lyla's heart echo

Dr. Suman seemed really taken with our daughter. He studied Lyla's X-rays, and we were relieved to learn she would need only an umbrella device to repair the hole in her heart. This particular procedure was far less invasive, and after one night of observation in the hospital, she would be free to go home—home as in get on the plane and fly to the United States!

First, Dr. Suman would verify his findings and decide whether her heart would take the umbrella device well. They would need to give her anesthesia and put an endoscope down her throat to look at her heart. So, that afternoon, we returned to the hospital and prepared Lyla for her trans esophageal echocardiogram. I was pretty nervous about handing her off to people I did not know. When the time came, it was indeed really hard for me to actually hand her off, but I had to trust and pray.

We walked up a flight of stairs to the Pediatric Intensive Care Unit (PICU) waiting area, which appeared more like a small lobby. There were tons of hospital employees coming in and out of the elevators and off the steps in this same area. An officer stood at the door to the PICU; no one could go back unless summoned by a doctor or nurse. The officer brought us plastic chairs to sit on, but he placed them in the middle of the "lobby" so that everyone had to walk around us. If big carts came through, we had to move. It just cracked me up how different things were compared to home, but overall the hospital was very efficient and clean, and we felt confident in our doctors.

While we waited on Lyla's test, sitting in our plastic chairs in the middle of the floor, another family arrived in the PICU waiting area. They were visibly worried and shaken. Scott offered his chair to the mom and discovered they spoke English. Their three-month-old son,

Shlok, was having emergency surgery on his heart. The surgery offered a 50% chance of survival rate. They were heartbroken for their little one. We prayed and shared Scriptures with them and talked to them about how Jesus was known for healing, and perhaps He would heal their son. Our prayer was that God would heal him so He would receive all the glory and this family could come to know Him personally. The mom told me she did not think God could hear her prayers, but when we showed up and prayed for her family, she knew He must be real. We exchanged numbers with them in hopes of hearing about God's healing of their baby boy. We asked our friends and family to pray for Shlok and his family as well.

After sitting there for a while, we were escorted like rock stars again, and everyone stared. The hospital staff placed us on the elevator before others who stood waiting in a line. We met with Dr. Suman, who informed us his diagnosis was confirmed; Lyla needed only the less-invasive umbrella device procedure. They would insert the device through an artery in her thigh, and there would be minimal pain; she would be under anesthesia again, but her recovery would be swift! He told us there was a two-percent chance it would not take, but not to worry. If for some reason it did not work, they would do the original open-heart surgery as planned.

"It is very rare for it not to work, and she could be playing football, running, and skipping soon," he assured us.

Lyla quickly became "the darling of the hospital;" all of the staff were in love with her. We were too. She would be admitted to the hospital on Tuesday night, and the procedure would be done on Wednesday morning.

When we saw Lyla in the PICU recovery room, we could see the anesthesia had taken a toll on her. She did not feel well and vomited a couple of times. Soon we were escorted to another small room, where we met with a hospital representative about payments and reserving a hospital room for her procedure. This was when we found out the hospital was going to charge us *double* the amount that we had negotiated before we came to India. We hoped to resolve the matter with Dr. Gopi in the morning, since he was busy in surgery with the little boy I mentioned earlier.

The next morning, Scott left for the hospital fairly early to speak with Dr. Gopi about the finances and how the hospital was charging us double the original agreement. He posted this on my blog:

> God has taught me so much through this process of adoption. He has shown me how much He is in control and how much I am not. I was so incredibly stressed about the potential for us to be charged double what we were anticipating for Lyla's surgery. It would be the difference of returning to the United States with a limited amount of debt versus returning home with significant credit card debt that would take several months, if not years, to pay off.
>
> When I left this morning to go work things out with the doctor, I had a sick feeling in my stomach. I have 5 children to care for. I can't properly care for them with a big credit card debt. My thoughts were racing. Why do I doubt God?
>
> For two hours I stood next to Dr. Gopi's office door, waiting for him. There was a very large crowd also sitting around me. His staff asked me to sit, but I refused. I prayed and read the Scriptures. God comforted me with passages of His sovereignty and His offer of peace. When Dr. Gopi came around the corner and saw me, he looked surprised.

He asked me what was wrong. I told him. He ushered me into his office and immediately got on his cell phone and office phone. Within minutes, three additional people were in his office. He told me not to worry about it. He said that our agreement was good. He told the others in his office to make it happen. I was relieved almost to tears. I was overwhelmed with God's provision.

I don't know if Dr. Gopi is a Christian, but I told him he was a gift from God to us. He began to chuckle. That is what Indians do when they are a bit nervous or embarrassed. I knew he took my words as a high compliment. They certainly were meant to be just that. I left the hospital feeling so weak and tired yet reveling in the mighty power of a great God whose provision is ever before me. When I returned to the hotel room, an anxious Kelly was waiting. Her questions were drowned out by the giggles and laughter of a little girl from Gujarat who was happy to see her daddy. When I consider how much I love her and how good God is, my heart can barely stand it. I don't know if I can physically stand to be any more blessed. My heart is overwhelmed.

Once again, God showed up. Well, technically He never left! And we desperately needed Him as another setback reared its ugly head. We received an e-mail from the orphanage stating they were unable to process her passport without her there in person. This was something we had quadruple checked with the orphanage before we left Ahmedabad. This meant an extended trip once again and more expenses in flights and hotel. But we clung to what we were reminded of that morning; God had seen us through this whole process, and He was showing no signs of leaving us.

Then our thoughts were no longer on our problems; we heard from Baby Shlok's father. Everything was still touch and go for them.

We checked into the hospital Tuesday night for some blood tests on Lyla to prepare for her procedure the following morning. We spent the night in her hospital room; Scott slept on a cot, and I slept with Lyla in her bed. I woke up in the middle of the night and saw Lyla in her sleep trying to pull her IV line out. I stopped her, but when we woke up, I could tell some of the pieces of her line were not connected properly.

Her tests showed she had a mild infection and her hemoglobin and iron were low. Therefore, instead of her umbrella device procedure, she needed to have a blood transfusion, which pushed back the umbrella device procedure another day. As we were talking with Dr. Suman, Lyla ripped the IV line out of her hand. She thought it was funny, while I thought I would have cried from the sting. We had to return to the PICU to get another IV line. She had her second line put in, and the nurses and doctor bragged that she didn't even shed a tear.

Dr. Gopi called Lyla "The People's Girl," as he told us how the entire hospital and community knew her and had concerns for her upcoming procedure. We continued to be very appreciative for the doctors and nurses who had shown such great love and care to our daughter and to our family!

While Lyla Ruth was in the PICU receiving her blood transfusion, Scott and I stepped out to run some errands. We were on a mission to see if we could purchase a dongle (portable Wi-Fi) to get better Internet access so we could communicate with the orphanage and find out what plan should be made regarding her passport. We were unable to get the portable Wi-Fi needed but did get to share the gospel with several people that day. We headed back to the hotel for reliable Internet and lunch. We confirmed with our agent and the orphanage we would indeed need to return to Ahmedabad, but we weren't sure when yet.

We ate lunch at the hotel, and Scott soon headed back to the hospital, while I stayed and showered. That would be my first time walking to the hospital by myself, but I needed to get some practice being alone because Scott would be gone soon.

The walk went fine; it just felt weird to be stared at by the people passing by. I kept smiling at all the women I saw, and they would smile back. Finally, I got to the hospital, but I had to cross a busy, chaotic street to get there, and I'm sure that was a big show for all the Indians sitting outside the hospital. I had a feeling they were making wagers on whether the white girl could make it across the street or not. It was like they had their own private viewing of the Atari game *Frogger*, and I was the frog. Anyone betting on me won! I made it.

Lyla still had not come back from the PICU, but when the nurses saw me, they asked me to go to the PICU because Lyla was calling for me. This made my heart jump to hear that she needed her Mom! Scott and I went together. They asked us to put on scrubs, which were on a rack outside the PICU door. The scrubs are used repeatedly. Once someone is finished with them, they are hung back on the rack. I had already worn some before, but for some reason it seemed harder this time. I guess knowing others had worn these same scrubs and the hats on their heads sent the lice fear into my head all over again. I told myself, parents will do anything for their children, right?

Lyla was all smiles when we walked in. It was also obvious to me the entire PICU staff, from the janitors to the doctors, were smitten with her. Every one of them could not walk by without talking to her and touching her. And, she reached out for them too.

Dr. Suman came in later and informed us there was still infection in her body, and he was not comfortable doing the procedure yet again. They ruled out a urinary tract infection but were still unaware of what and where the infection was because she simply did not act sick. Dr. Suman cautioned us if he did this procedure while she had an infection, it could be very dangerous and would possibly require open heart surgery. He was nervous about telling us this, because he knew we were anxious to get back home as quickly as possible. However, we reassured him we wanted what was best for our daughter, and he was relieved. Now the procedure was moved to Friday. She would spend Thursday taking stronger antibiotics to kill off the infection.

We were stuck in the hospital room all day Thursday. I had never come up with more creative ways to play with a four-year-old while cooped up in a hospital room in my life. I mean, there were only so many places to hide for hide-and-seek. One thing I tried to do was work on her walking skills. Lyla reached up and wanted to be held a lot; I wanted her to become more comfortable with walking. It was apparent she had never been given the opportunity to be active and to build strength and coordination. I imagined her being put in a spot and told to stay there. But she was "running" free now. Scott and I could not get over how much her walking had improved in one week. She still had stiffness in her legs when she walked but was getting faster. She still could not walk on her tippy-toes, run, or jump. We played lots of games where we would walk as fast as we could from one side of the room to the other. We did some squats, marches around the room, and danced a lot. I tried to engage her in as much physical activity as possible.

Her behavior was a little rough that day. It was hard to find the right way to discipline her. Scott and I felt she was probably used to a very strict environment in the orphanage, where she lived in fear of messing up. But when she got to us, perhaps she found this new freedom exhilarating and tried to push all of the boundaries. It was difficult because we had no structure with our schedule and our location. Not being able to communicate with her through language made it even more difficult. However, I knew she understood what "no" meant, but she would choose to continue doing whatever she was doing anyway. It was a struggle to find the balance between loving her and applying the correct discipline with all the various factors involved while penned up in a room all day; it was super boring for her and for me!

Another concern that developed concerned Lyla's lack of regard for stranger-danger or meeting new people. She showed signs of what is called "Indiscriminate Friendliness or Affection."[27] She had no trouble hugging complete strangers, running up to the various workers in the hospital, reaching out to waiters at restaurants—or to anyone she came across, for that matter. Most everyone around us found it endearing and would comment on how sweet she was. However, Scott and I knew better. We had read about this and how common it is in post-adoption behavior in internationally adopted children. They will do anything to get attention and to feel loved. All the books and articles we had read instructed parents to limit

27 Boris Gindis, Ph.D., "Post-Orphanage Behavior in Internationally Adopted Children," *Center for Cognitive-Developmental Assessment & Remediation*, April 20, 2012, http://bgcenter.com/BGPublications/orphanagebehavior.htm.

the interactions of others with their child—grandparents included—until bonding between the nuclear family had grown stronger.

Our circumstances didn't allow us to practice this advice. It was also difficult to communicate with others why we were trying to teach her not to hug or run to strangers. It seemed when we tried to discipline Lyla for initiating hugs and kisses with others, "the others" would get offended.

We compared Lyla's overt responses to how our own children responded to strangers and determined that, although our children are friendly, not one of them would run up to strangers and hug or kiss them—especially not Katy Pierce. In public places, she usually wanted to be close to Mommy or Daddy, and this feeling intensified when strangers, or even friends, came near to her; she would cling even closer to us. It was clear to us Lyla was struggling in this department, and we struggled to help her find the balance of being friendly versus seeking attention.

Regardless of these issues, we were madly in love with Lyla! We were learning more and more about her each day. She was such a chatterbox. She talked to us like we knew exactly what she was saying, and she had the cutest little voice. She was high energy and a major people person. She wanted to be near someone at all times. She was funny, always making silly faces and acting silly.

We discovered our little Lyla was a tattletale. One time as she was eating her dinner, and I took a bite of it; she went and told on me to Scott, talking and pointing as she chattered on. I took another bite to see what she would do, and she ran and told on me again. When I quit eating her food, she offered me a bite, and then when I ate it, she ran to tattle again. This kid cracked me up. All I could think about was how much she and her siblings were going to love being with each other. She would be able to fit right in with all my other tattletales.

As I mentioned before, everyone was fascinated with our adoption here. We were "big time" in Hyderabad! Each day we gave an interview about our adoption with some type of news venue. People asked us questions like why did we choose India? How did we choose our daughter? Why did we choose Star Hospital?

Dr. Gopi has a local foundation similar to Babyheart called the Hrudaya Foundation. That particular afternoon, we had a television interview, and our story was on the local news.

Three different doctors came by the room that night to confirm that the procedure would take place the next day, on Friday morning. Baby Shlok's mom also came by our room. Dr. Gopi had told us earlier that he was doing better. Shlok's mom said all our prayers were working and she hoped he would be moved into Lyla's PICU unit tomorrow, which meant there was a chance we could all be in there together. Baby Shlok had a long way to full recovery.

Friday morning finally arrived. I escorted Lyla up to the PICU. From the PICU, we were placed into a sort of holding room with six beds. Five of the beds had older men in them, and the sixth bed was for Lyla. Being in that room made me nervous because the men seemed to be really sick, the floors did not look very clean, and neither did the sheet on her bed. It made me uncomfortable, and I knew she was uncomfortable too, because she wanted me to hold her. I held her as long as they would let me. There was one nurse who came in that was making a fuss about my being there. I'm not sure if it was my presence or the fact I was wearing the scrubs but not one of those little scrub hats, as I had gotten lucky. They were all being used, and there wasn't one left out in the hall on the rack.

I almost asked for the nurse's name to report her rudeness to Dr. Gopi. Instead, I took a deep breath to calm down; I knew my nerves were stretched thin over the room as well as the procedure. I also reminded myself she had been the only rude person we had encountered in the hospital. All of the staff had been warm, hospitable, and helpful to us. However, I think she was the reason the nurses indicated I needed to join Scott in the lobby area.

Lyla did not want me to go and grabbed my shirt. I tried to be all smiley and tell her it was all going to be okay and that I would see her in a little while. After we kissed good-bye, I headed toward the door. Glancing back, I saw her cocker-spaniel-sad-eye look that had been part of all her pictures. I told myself to be strong as she needed to see I was okay with the situation. I put on a happy face, blew her a kiss, and walked out.

Then I quickly took the shared scrubs off and headed back to our room. I thought I was going to break down and cry, but God poured peace and comfort all over me, and I knew He was going to be with Lyla.

When I got to our room, Scott and I prayed. Then a nurse came in and said, "They need you on the 4th floor, the case is about to happen."

Not really sure what they meant, we headed up to the 4th floor. We were told to put on the shared scrubs once again. Like I said before, anything for my babies! We were ushered by security to the same room with the six beds. I could see Lyla through a window as we approached; she was crying hysterically in the arms of a nurse. When she saw us, she reached out for me, and I went and took her in my arms. Other nurses asked for her, but she did not want to leave me. This may sound selfish, but I was comforted by the fact I was the only one who could calm her.

Dr. Suman walked in with the anesthesiologist. He reached for her, and she did go to him. She loved Dr. Suman! It was an additional comfort for me too, to see a familiar face.

Dr. Suman informed us the procedure should take about an hour, and then she would be in the PICU in recovery for quite a while. We told Dr. Suman we would be praying for him, and he said, "Of course," with his sweet smile and his Indian head bob. The head bob is their way to say yes while tilting their head side to side instead of front to back. It takes a few days to get used to, but I found myself doing it along with them!

We hugged and kissed Lyla one more time before she and Dr. Suman walked out the other side of the room. She looked back, and I blew her a kiss. We left for breakfast and met up with a new friend from the States to visit for a little while.

Shortly after her procedure, we were able to see Lyla in the PICU. She started crying when she saw me, wanting to be held. I was not allowed to pick her up, but I could hold her hand and rub her head. She got calmer while I was there. Scott went in after me, because we could go in only one at a time. We also met with the doctor, who said everything looked successful, and there were no glitches with her procedure. He even showed us a video of her procedure. Praise God! We could have her back in our room later that afternoon.

A few hours later, we received a phone call from the PICU, telling us that Lyla was crying again. We hurried back to the hospital and peeked through the door; she was sitting up in her bed and not crying at all. As soon as she saw us, the tears began to fall. She was ready to get out of that room and back to her hospital room; she kept begging for us to take her out. She was saying it in Gujarati, but I knew exactly what she wanted. We couldn't leave until the Sisters (nurses) said we could.

At last they granted permission. The moment Lyla was wheeled out of the PICU, she was content. It was apparent she did not feel well; she was very groggy and moody and quiet. Her little grin did manage to show through a few times. Of course, while we were out in the hall, everyone had to touch her and poke at her. They were showing their affection to her. After all, she was the "People's Girl," as Dr. Gopi expressed earlier.

We got back to our hospital room, and she met our friend Eve.[28] Eve gave her a new pair of shoes, and Lyla immediately put them on. She loved shoes! I think she was fascinated with shoes because she probably never had a pair of her own. Eve went straight to her heart with that gift! Lyla was also hungry, and Daddy helped feed her. She wasn't acting like herself completely, and they gave her some pain medicine to help her nap and continue to recover. Dr. Suman felt like we would be discharged from the hospital the next morning.

Another special thing had happened that day; when we went into the PICU, lying in the bed next to Lyla was Baby Shlok. He had been taken to our PICU, which was a good sign for his health. However, he was still in very fragile condition. We were able to see him and pray over him. While I was out in the hall, his mom walked up, exhausted and worried. She said the doctor told her it would be at least a week before they could give her any kind of hope or good news. I hugged

---

28 Name changed for security purposes.

her and told her we were all praying, and I asked if we could pray with her in our room tonight.

As the day went on, especially closer to dinnertime, Lyla became her old self again, playing, laughing, and squealing. She was taken back upstairs for an echocardiogram, to check out the functioning of the device. They said it looked great and she would be 100% healthy. The doctor even said, "She will probably even start to get chubby in the next few weeks." He said she had definitely been showing signs of anemia, but she should be better now. She had to start a medication regimen; for the next six months, she would have to take a pill to prevent blood clots in her heart around the device. But after that, she should be good to go! The doctors wanted to see her one more time in the morning, and then we could be discharged!

The next morning, we bought some chocolates as gifts for the Sisters who had taken care of Lyla. We went ahead and said our good-byes to them. They were very appreciative, and all of them were taking pictures with Lyla.

We also got to visit with Baby Shlok's parents one more time. They came by our room, and through many tears, we were able to pray with them. The night before, they received a call from the hospital saying that Shlok had to be placed on a ventilator once again. They were heartbroken, tired, and longing for answers. We talked for a while and encouraged them to reach out to God during the process. As they were leaving, we hugged and prayed one more time. I felt the Lord nudging me to give Shlok's mom one of my most favorite possessions ever: *The Power of the Praying Parent,* a book by Stormie Omartian. I felt like I was handing over one of my children! That book had been with me since Seth was born and had been my spiritual playbook as I grew as a parent. I hoped that Shlok's mom would read it and find truth and comfort in the prayers and Scriptures as I had.

I jokingly said to Scott I didn't realize we were on a mission trip or that "Pastor Scott" would have to fulfill pastoral duties and make hospital visits while he was here. But truthfully, I stood amazed at God and His sovereignty and how our paths had crossed with certain people in Ahmedabad and Hyderabad. One day, I want Lyla to know God used her adoption and her surgery to reach people for Him. I wondered how He was going to use us back in Ahmedabad when we returned for the passport, and also in New Delhi, the last leg of our trip. I was excited to see!

It was a good reminder for me: no matter where we are, God wants to use His people. We don't have to be on a mission trip or going through an adoption to be used by Him. We witnessed to two couples because of everyday life. The first one was the family we sat beside in a hallway while waiting on a doctor; the other while we were getting service for Internet at a phone company. Anyone could do this! My prayer is that all of God's people would be sensitive to the needs of others around us, no matter where we are each day!

Right before we finished being discharged, the hospital brought their media team in and interviewed us with cameras one last time. (I told you we had made it big there!) As we made our way out of the room, the hospital staff presented Lyla with flowers. God was so faithful to send us to Star Hospital! We headed back to the hotel room to crash.

The next day, we had our final check up with Dr. Suman at the hospital. When Lyla saw him, she ran to him. She adored him, and I must say we did too. Not only was he a fabulous doctor, but he was also a wonderful person with a huge heart for children. In the past week, we had learned more about him. In his spare time, he volunteered out in the villages, providing medical care. He also personally sponsored orphan girls in Hyderabad. He pays for them to go to school and sees to it all of their needs are met. He showed us pictures of a few of them on his phone, as proud of them as if they were his own children.

He did one last echocardiogram, which showed us the device in Lyla's heart, and it was functioning properly. He gave us an iron supplement for Lyla to take daily to build up her hemoglobin and iron levels. When our visit wound down, we made sure we had each other's contact information. We hoped to always keep in touch with Dr. Suman and Dr. Gopi. We were so thankful for God putting them in our lives and for saving our daughter's life and future!

After the checkup, I spent all afternoon with our new friend Eve. She took me shopping, and I loaded up on spices and mixes to bring home to make Indian food.

After a fun girls' day, I entered the hotel room. Lyla was super excited to see me. That made my day! We had one final meal at the hotel before we packed up to head back to Ahmedabad the next morning. We couldn't get Lyla's passport issues resolved soon enough. I was anxious to get her home and introduce her to her new siblings.

Some new friends in Ahmedabad, strangers really, were picking us up at the airport and allowing us to stay in their home until I had the passport in my hand. Yet another one of God's provisions! God's family and His hospitality through them stretched across the world!

Chapter 12

THE LIFE SHE HAD

WE MADE OUR VERY EARLY 3:45 A.M. morning plane ride back to Ahmedabad to resolve our passport issues. Scott and I had mixed emotions about the whole passport process in Ahmedabad. We were mainly nervous for Lyla and how she would feel seeing Mr. Pandit again. We didn't want her to think we were giving her back.

Our new friend Sarah and her sweet daughter Grace[29] met us at the airport, and we went back to their house and chatted for a while. Sarah made us a delicious omelet. Lyla loved playing with all of Grace's toys. Grace was five and so sweet to share her dolls. We also met Sarah's husband, Thomas, and their very polite seven-year-old son, Noah.[30] Sarah reminded us so much of our friend Andrea back home. In fact, I almost called her by the wrong name several times. They both are very active, super prayer warriors, crafty, and parent similarly.

Of course, we let them know we appreciated their incredible hospitality. They took in a family of strangers, and we wanted to

---

29 Names changed for security purposes.
30 Names changed for security purposes.

contribute toward groceries and gas because they were helping us save a ton of money from hotel fees, autos, and food.

Thomas proceeded to tell us a story. Their family had been reading a children's version of *Pilgrim's Progress* together. I believe he said they read a chapter a few days earlier where the main character, Christian, and his friends were weary from traveling, and he came upon the home of a man named Gaius. Gaius, who is also mentioned in 3 John in the Bible, opened his home to the strangers. The Christians asked how they could repay him for his food, shelter, and kindness. But Gaius refused any payment and continued to serve them as his honored guests. He offered all that he had and did not withhold anything, as unto the Lord.

Thomas said his family discussed Gaius and the importance of opening one's home and of sacrificial giving as a family. He said, "The very next morning you called and asked if we had room for you in our home." He knew God had ordained the timing of my call, and now their family was able to demonstrate and live out what they read. They were opening their home to strangers weary from travel and providing all they had without withholding anything.

> The Pastor, to my good friend Gaius: How truly I love you! We're the best of friends, and I pray for good fortune in everything you do, and for your good health—that your everyday affairs prosper, as well as your soul! I was most happy when some friends arrived and brought the news that you persist in following the way of Truth. Nothing could make me happier than getting reports that my children continue diligently in the way of Truth!
>
> Dear friend, when you extend hospitality to Christian brothers and sisters, even when they are strangers, you

make the faith visible. They've made a full report back to the church here, a message about your love. It's good work you're doing, helping these travelers on their way, hospitality worthy of God himself! They set out under the banner of the Name, and get no help from unbelievers. So they deserve any support we can give them. In providing meals and a bed, we become their companions in spreading the Truth (3 John 1:1–8, The Message).

This family's ministry to my immediate family caused me to consider my own heart toward others. Am I reflecting the hospitality that Christ wants me to? May I choose not to hold possessions, my home, or my own personal space too close. After all, those things already belong to Jesus anyway. Everything I have, has come from Him. And this I know (and am fully reminded of while in India): I am richly blessed with material items, shelter, and food when compared to most people in the world. Thank You, God, for giving me all of these things. Please give me an opportunity to use them for You!

After getting to know our new friends who said we could stay as long as we needed (praise God!), we made the dreaded trip back to the orphanage. I could tell by his body language and the deep breaths he was taking that Scott was anxious and nervous for Lyla. This time, on the other hand, I had a supernatural peace come over me, and I was doing fine. Sarah said a very sweet prayer over us in the car that brought much comfort before she drove us to the orphanage.

God's timing is always glorious and perfect, and as His timing would have it, Lyla fell asleep in the car. She was exhausted from our long trip. When we arrived at the orphanage, she was out of it. We spent hardly a minute at the orphanage because Mr. Pandit was ready to get to the passport office. We were actually a little late getting to him because the traffic was so bad that morning. (In retrospect, it was more of God's timing.)

So we quickly got back in Sarah's car and headed for the passport office. She handled driving in Indian traffic like a real pro. The passport office ended up being only five minutes away from where Thomas and Sarah lived. However, the orphanage was on the other side of the city.

We arrived at the passport office, and Lyla had awakened. She saw Mr. Pandit but seemed fine. She was especially clingy to Scott and me but did not seem upset by seeing him. I think being sleepy helped her.

Mr. Pandit reached for her, and she denied him. He made a comment that she was really bonded to us. "She has crossed over to your side. She no longer come to my side. She go to your side only."

I just beamed with pride and thought to myself, *Dang straight! That's MY girl!*

When we went into the office, Mr. Pandit entered the room as if he ran the place. He motioned for us to come, and we followed him around as he bypassed lines and those waiting in them. We later learned from Thomas that the name *Pandit* is a name in a very high caste in India, so technically he could do most anything he wanted. He took us behind some glass walls that separated us from the rest of the crowd. We waited only a few minutes and went into a small office where a passport official took Lyla's thumbprint and photo and scanned all of the necessary papers.

Mr. Pandit said we would more than likely get the passport next Monday. We were desperately hoping this was real time and not Indian time, as Indians seem to move much slower than Westerners.

They did have some holidays coming up that week that could potentially delay the process even longer. At the passport office, we chatted a little more with Mr. Pandit and asked him more questions about Lyla, and I also asked if I could return to the orphanage and take more pictures of the children. Mr. Pandit wanted us to come the next day at 5:00 PM for chai and cookies. Then he would tell us all about the orphanage, and Lyla and I could take some pictures. We did find out that the orphanage was home to 100 children. I was sort of shocked to hear that number, and at the same time, I remembered how large the facility was, so they could certainly house that number adequately.

The next morning, our host family continued to shower us with hospitality, serving a delicious breakfast and a yummy lunch. We spent some time shopping and hanging out with Lyla and continuing to get to know her better.

Her behavior was a bit of a battle that day. She had pushed every button imaginable. She even had four major crying fits when she didn't get her way. In my mind it was such a war as I tried to pick my battles wisely and also balance teaching her who was in charge and that she couldn't have everything she wanted. I felt like sometimes all we said was "no" to her because it was one of the words we both understand fully. It was hard for me to accept because I didn't always want to be negative.

It was the little things that became annoying, like her thinking it was funny to put her feet on the table, to not wanting to nap, to refusing to wear her shoes (and that is rare since she loves shoes, which is another reason I knew she was being defiant), to wanting to touch everything in a store. She behaved like most kids I know, but it was a tough transition day for her.

Scott and I took turns sitting with her or near her as she went through her fits. Again, it was another spiritual analogy for me. It reminded me of my spiritual walk. There is so much freedom in knowing and loving Christ, yet there are boundaries and standards set for our spiritual benefit, even sometimes our physical benefit. As a Christian, sometimes I push those boundaries and have crying fits when I don't get my way. God showed me again how He sits with me and waits patiently, even when I throw fit after fit.

Thankfully, Sarah asked if she could watch Lyla for us while we went back to the orphanage that afternoon. On the car ride to the orphanage, my mind was wandering everywhere. I was anxious to hear more of Lyla's story and learn all I could about the life she once had, and I was determined to get pictures of other children in the orphanage that were matched with the families I knew. Earlier that day, I received two additional messages from families I didn't know personally, asking if I could try to see their kids too. I was delighted to do that for them. I knew I would wish for the same if the roles were reversed. I hoped to take pictures for five different families.

When we arrived, we waited only a few minutes for Mr. Pandit. We were sitting in the main lobby where it all started for us in the orphanage. Lots of activity was happening; our friend Thomas went with us to help translate and to check out the orphanage. He said because it was the first day of the month, there was a lot of business to be done.

We chatted with Mr. Pandit for about twenty minutes. First, he told us the history of the orphanage and all they offer the children there. It has been operating since 1892. Then he told us how lucky we were, because India had recently changed some of its adoption guidelines while we were in the process. But thankfully, we were far enough along that we did not get affected like some other cases. He was telling us how we had just escaped the changes that make it harder for foreigners to adopt from India.

What he said next, I will always cherish and never forget: He said we were also lucky because when he put our daughter's information out for agencies to show interested families, there were families all over the world interested in her. Families from Austria, Mexico, Canada, America, Portugal, and Spain wanted to be matched with her, but we had accepted her referral just in time. This was amazing to me, since it took us at least a week to make a decision because we were trying so hard to work out her heart surgery issues first. It really did my heart good to hear all those other people wanted her, but we were the ones that got her! Mr. Pandit kept calling it luck, but I knew differently. It was all God's doing and His orchestrated plan—His perfect plan.

Mr. Pandit told us he had our daughter since she was a baby. She was in a village in Bharuch and then brought into town to a police station. The police station placed her with a different orphanage, but that orphanage felt they could not care for her because of her heart issue. Mr. Pandit asked them to please bring her to his orphanage. And this was where she spent the next four years of her life. From information we'd been able to piece together, she had been in this orphanage since she was four months old.

We asked about how the local Indians felt about adoption, and he said he gets tons of requests. They have so many requests that they allow the nationals to come only once a week in a four-hour window. This was refreshing to learn, yet he still had 100 kids in his orphanage. He also told us out of the 100 children, there are 95 girls and 5 boys. My friend's son Ajay was one of them.

I asked about Lyla's given name *Ami*—where it derived from and its meaning. Mr. Pandit told us he had been the one to name her. He explained the name Ami meant a pleasant feeling, and he used the example of eating a wonderful meal and how you feel afterwards. Using a food association with our family is great, because we love to eat! But it was just an example; he was trying to describe the feeling. I imagine it more as the pleasant sensation one feels when full of the Holy Spirit and the Peace of Christ within. We were definitely keeping *Ami* as part of her name.

I remembered the worry and concern I had over renaming her, how I prayed God would make what we should do clear to us. He did! The first day we met Lyla and were in our hotel room, I called out "Lyla" when her back was turned, and she turned to look at me as if that had been her name all along. And she has never looked back. She has been Lyla ever since, our sweet and feisty Lyla Ruth Ami Parkison.

After our chat, we were escorted into the same little room next to the office where we had spent time on our first visit. There was an elderly Indian woman in there, and she wanted to know all about Lyla's surgery and how she was doing now. She was the madame secretary of the orphanage. She told us her husband helped build the complex. The men at the orphanage and Mr. Pandit showed her a great deal of respect. We took some pictures with her and asked if we could take a tour of the facility.

My heart was pounding as they discussed it. I didn't know if they let people tour the orphanage much. I was very much hoping they would allow it so we could see what Lyla's life was like in the early years. Besides, I had all those families counting on me!

Mr. Pandit agreed. We started off by going to the computer lab, a room with about fifteen desktop computers. Next we walked across the courtyard. As we were walking, a group of children looked over the balcony on the second level, waving and smiling. I immediately spotted Ajay and Smita in the crowd. I hollered to them and gave them a big wave and hello. They just smiled, laughed, and waved.

Then we saw the kitchen and the dining hall. He said they ring a bell, and the kids come running. We looked at the kitchen; Mr. Pandit was very proud of the freezers they had. He explained that all of the children sit in four long rows down the dining hall. They sit on the floor, and I assume they use their fingers to eat. After all, it's the Indian way.

As we walked out of the dining hall, I looked over to the right and saw about six older girls sitting outside. They hardly acknowledged us. I looked up to my left, and on the second floor there were a group of tween girls waving and smiling. I was scanning the area for all of my friends' children. Then we started back toward the offices. I was thinking the tour might be coming to an end, but we took a left and climbed a set of stairs.

I soon learned at the top of this stairway were the rooms where Lyla spent her time in the orphanage. Three rooms were there, all connected with glass walls. The bottom half of the wall was like a regular wall, but the top half was glass, so adults could see in or across. We first went into the nursery. There were three tiny babies, smaller than any of my biological babies when they were first born. Mr. Pandit told me one of the babies was being adopted. The nursery appeared to be very clean and safe. Everything was sterile—no toys, colors, or any type of decorations. It was very quiet and calm.

The next room was a mid-way room for babies starting to walk and crawl. There were only two children in here. In this room I saw Sakshi for the first time. There were two families I had connected with via the Internet from Ireland, and she would belong to one of them. She was a beautiful child, younger than Lyla, with a cute round face. She appeared to be a little bit chubbier than Lyla. I was beginning to see more evidence of how Lyla's heart condition de-layed her growth and development. Sakshi was holding the hand of a caretaker and waddling around. It was special to see my friends' daughter. I was rejoicing inside because I knew she had parents that were going to love her like crazy, and they should be there within the next two months.

However, it was the next child that just broke my heart. It was a little boy in a walker. He appeared to be about two or three. I could tell by his legs he had some sort of deformity or special need. He looked very feeble. But he had a beautiful face with big, beautiful round eyes. His walker was tied to the wall so he could not really go anywhere. Mr. Pandit informed me he had been turned down many times because he had thalassemia, which is a blood disorder. I ap-proached the child and got down on his level. I reached out for his hand, and his eyes lit up. I could tell he enjoyed having a friend talk to him. It was all I could do not to burst into tears right then and there. My heart was so broken for him. I hope the caretakers love on him, and I prayed God would raise up a family for this boy. I can't even finish this sentence without tears streaming down my face. He deserves a family just like a healthy child.

The next room had older kids (up to age four) and children that seemed a little more mobile. There were about eight children in there, and Sakshi and her caretaker followed us in there too. I was thinking they use both rooms for the kids that are in the walking/crawling stage. In this room, I was determined to find other children that were in the process of being adopted by other friends in the United States I have met via the Internet. I found one. The precious child was sitting on the floor and watching us. This child is blind in one eye, yet oh so cute. I was thankful I got to see the child and relay info back to the mom.

All of the children in this area stared at us with somber expressions, much like my little Lyla when we first met her. I think we were frightening in some ways because they probably rarely see white people there, and we are so much taller than they are, even much taller than their caretakers. Again, all of the rooms looked very clean and safe, but they had no life in them. There was no color, no decorations, and not many toys.

Mr. Pandit also mentioned there were two other children with a thyroid disorder in that room that had been denied by families. It was heart wrenching to hear. I know God has parents out there for these special children!

We left the nursery area. Down below, waiting on us in the courtyard area, were bright-eyed and giddy Ajay and Smita. These kids were nothing but smiles and so beautiful! I snapped lots of pictures. Then Ajay asked in Gujarati when we were going to take him home. I knew this might happen, and the Carrolls and I had already discussed that it might be confusing for them to see us, but I asked Mr. Pandit to please explain that we are their parents' friends, and his parents are coming very soon.

Scott and I felt horrible, and we frantically searched for pictures of Amanda and Jeff, their parents, on our iPad and camera, because we had a recent visit with them in August. Unfortunately, I had already deleted them off the devices. I think I must have said out loud, "It's too bad we can't FaceTime." Scott replied, "Let's give it a try!" We started looking for Wi-Fi but were unsuccessful. However, our friend Thomas offered his cell phone as a hot spot, and we got wireless right there, and we were able to FaceTime with Amanda!

FaceTiming with Amanda

It was such an incredible sight to see. I witnessed Amanda see her kids and talk to them for the first time in person, and the kids were so happy and calling her Mommy. It did my heart some good to know they could recognize that she was their Mom. They enjoyed seeing their future rooms and most of all loved seeing their future dog, Willow. They were laughing and holding hands with each other. They were such sweet siblings who were going to join two other sweet siblings soon! We probably spent a good 45 minutes with them.

During this time I also saw Minal, my other Irish friend's daughter. She is a little younger than Lyla but walking very well; she, too had more meat on her bones in a healthy way and was very sweet and beautiful. They told her to pick me a flower. When she handed it to me, she did not smile very much. She had that same confused stare the other children have had, but she warmed up to us as time went on. By default, the caretakers and Mr. Pandit got distracted with the whole FaceTime thing, and Minal stayed with us for a good 45 minutes.

Unfortunately, I did not get to see two other children whose families were hoping I could take pictures and visit with them. Our tour was coming to an end. There were some highs and lows for me, and my emotions had run their course for the day. As we were leaving, we stopped in the lobby where we first saw Lyla. Some policemen carried a tiny baby into the orphanage. When I saw the baby, I could not hold my emotions any longer. I started crying uncontrollably. Tears dripped off my face onto the marble floor. I told Thomas I needed to leave. My heart was heavy dealing with everything I had seen and experienced.

It took me quite a while to process our visit to the orphanage. I was thankful to see where Lyla lived most of her days and to know it was clean and safe. But I also knew an institution was still an institution; nothing compares to having a loving parent. My heart was broken over the special needs children and for the older girls who may never be adopted because of their age.

I think ultimately I developed a greater appreciation and understanding of Lyla's journey into our family. Obviously, God ordained it and had his hand on her from the very beginning of her life. Remember, she was born in a different town and originally placed at a different orphanage, but God brought her here at a specific time to be chosen by us. Remember, there were six other families that wanted her, but we claimed her first. I sat in awe of an awesome God who had been with Lyla from the very beginning. At that moment, Psalm 139 came to mind:

O LORD, you have searched me and known me!
You know when I sit down and when I rise up;
you discern my thoughts from afar.
You search out my path and my lying down
and are acquainted with all my ways.
Even before a word is on my tongue,
behold, O LORD, you know it altogether.
You hem me in, behind and before,
and lay your hand upon me.
Such knowledge is too wonderful for me;
it is high; I cannot attain it.

Where shall I go from your Spirit?
Or where shall I flee from your presence?
If I ascend to heaven, you are there!
If I make my bed in Sheol, you are there!
If I take the wings of the morning
and dwell in the uttermost parts of the sea,
even there your hand shall lead me,
and your right hand shall hold me.
If I say, "Surely the darkness shall cover me,
and the light about me be night,"
even the darkness is not dark to you;
the night is bright as the day,
for darkness is as light with you.
For you formed my inward parts;
you knitted me together in my mother's womb.
I praise you, for I am fearfully and wonderfully made.

Wonderful are your works;
my soul knows it very well.
My frame was not hidden from you,
when I was being made in secret,
intricately woven in the depths of the earth.
Your eyes saw my unformed substance;
in your book were written, every one of them,
the days that were formed for me,
when as yet there was none of them.
How precious to me are your thoughts, O God!
How vast is the sum of them!
If I would count them, they are more than the sand.
I awake, and I am still with you.

~ Psalm 139: 1–18, ESV

The next day was Scott's last day in India. He needed to return to the States to get back to work, and we were happy he was getting back to our other children. Lyla and I were going to miss him greatly, but one thing I would not miss about Scott—riding India's old rickety elevators with him. He jumped up and down and shook them and scared everyone riding. Nope, I would not miss that!

Shortly before Scott left, we received a text from Baby Shlok's father. "I praise the Almighty for the positive trend in Shlok's health. He should be getting off the ventilator this week, and the swelling in his heart has gone down."

We praised God together for healing Shlok. We also prayed for Lyla's passport to arrive on Monday, so we could join Scott at home soon.

The next few days were spent connecting with Lyla on a deeper level. I learned more about her: She's a lefty; she loves chocolate chip cookies; she is a good sleeper; she has a birthmark on her back; she swings her right arm excessively when she walks; she does not like any juice drinks; she loves taking bucket baths; and she likes to put things in her mouth like a toddler.

My new friend Sarah knew I was ready to be home with my whole family. Hence, she provided wonderful distractions and activities for us each day to pass the time quickly during our stay. Sarah took us shopping, to play at an indoor playground, to Indian cooking lessons, to McDonald's, to Bible studies, and to run errands. While it helped to pass the time, I also enjoyed getting to know her and her family on a deeper level too. Hearing about their ministry and watching them do life in Ahmedabad was fascinating to me.

Navratri, a ten-day festival in India, started while I was there. Thomas and Sarah warned me in advance about the noise and loud music that would be playing at night and in the early morning hours. I watched from the rooftop terrace of our apartment building on the first night of the festival. I watched the members of the apartment complex perform their puja (worship ceremonies). They had to wake their god; they offered food to the idol, and one by one each person would perform their own personal puja to the idol. After puja, they celebrated with clapping, singing, and dancing. There was extremely loud music playing outside until about 2:00 A.M. It was truly beautiful to watch all the dance formations and customs but sad to know it was all for a statue that their local idol maker carved with his hands and delivered that day. I prayed for God to reach these people.

I desired for us all to be dancing and clapping together around the throne of God in heaven one day!

I attended a Christian church with my friends the next morning. It was a Hindi speaking service. Even though I had no idea what they were singing, it seemed to be some of the most genuine worship I had ever experienced. I knew at one point they were singing a song to the King, because I heard the name Raja. They were lifting their hands in the air and smiling. Some of them were even dancing a little. But they were truly dancing for the one true God, quite the transition from last night's dancing. I teared up watching them, desiring to worship with sincerity and to be filled with that kind of joy each Sunday.

I often take for granted the gift we've been given in worshipping with our church family and singing praises unto the Lord. These Christian Indians truly knew what it meant to walk in darkness and find the light. They knew firsthand what persecution was like, and they still loved God with all their might.

Another spiritual observation I had was that the men worshipped with such enthusiasm. The women were also joyful, but the men were the most expressive. I loved seeing men be the spiritual leaders in worship, and for all of the children present to see them worshipping God. I think sometimes (not all of the time) it is flipped in America. It seems our men are more reserved and private about their worship and the women are more open and expressive. It was really special to see it in reverse.

I had high hopes of Lyla's passport arriving on Monday, but around lunchtime that day, I was notified the passport was still in process of being printed and would *maybe* be ready Tuesday. I was riding in the car with my friends, doing my best to hold it together. Sarah looked at me and asked, "Are you okay?"

Tears started flowing. I said through sobs, "I just want to see my other children. I miss them!" Immediately they started praying and encouraging me. Additionally, they took me to do what every girl needs to do after being a little sad: we ate some chocolate and shopped a little.

Later that evening after Lyla was in bed, I chatted with my friends' house helper, Ravina.[31] I had gotten to know her during my stay in Ahmedabad. She told me a little about her life, and much of it was sad. She mentioned there were times she wished she could die.

I already knew that my friends had been sharing the gospel with her regularly, so she had some knowledge about eternity and Jesus. "I don't want you to die, especially without knowing where you would go when you die!" I told her.

She paused and then replied, "I want to accept Him, but I do not know how."

I told her the Bible says, "If you confess with your mouth that Jesus is Lord, and believe in your heart that God raised him from the dead, you will be saved" (Rom. 10:9, ESV).

That instant, she held up her hands and said, "Jesus is Lord!"

I knew she was ready; I hoped Sarah would join us soon from putting her kids to bed; she had been pouring spiritually into Ravina for quite some time, and I wanted her to be there. Sarah joined us at just the right time. I explained the situation, and Sarah and Ravina prayed together. I gained a new sister in Christ!

---

31 Name changed for security purposes.

After my day of disappointment from not getting the passport, God brought something to my mind. I remembered earlier in the car, when I was crying, I had silently prayed, "Lord, use me while I am here, since I can't be at home." Suddenly, I realized He had done just that. If that passport had been ready, there was a good chance my conversation with Ravina would have never happened. Ravina had been poured into spiritually by the family there. God placed me at the right place at the right time to be a part of Ravina's salvation story. The next day, I awoke with such a joy over my new sister in Christ that I was no longer concerned about when that passport was going to make it.

It was monsoon season in Ahmedabad, and it rained quite a bit over the next few days. I actually saw a car under water up to the tops of its tires! We didn't do much that day because it was one of those stay-inside-and-listen-to-the-rain days.

Lyla and I played with Legos for a while to pass the time, and she and sweet little Grace played together. She even gave Lyla some of her Indian clothes and some precious pink high heels to keep. Needless to say, Lyla loved them. The passport still had not arrived, but I trusted God's timing and plan was best.

The next afternoon, I received the anticipated phone call. The passport had arrived at the orphanage. I picked it up with relief to finally have it in hand. I quickly made reservations to fly to New Delhi the next morning. But, as excited as I was to be a step closer to home, I was going to miss my dear new friends and gracious hosts who had taken such great care of us during our stay. We said our good-byes that night, as Lyla and I had a very early morning flight to catch.

The next morning we headed to New Delhi, where several major tasks needed to be completed before heading home. Lyla was required to undergo two medical examinations for her travel visa. We would also have to get her visa from the Embassy, and we would have an out-processing interview with the Embassy about our adoption.

Thankfully, another family, the Smiths,[32] graciously agreed to take us in during our stay in New Delhi, another big blessing! Again, Lyla and I arrived that morning as strangers and hoped to depart (like last time) as friends! This family had three children very close in age to my children at home. When we arrived at the Smiths' home, we stayed only long enough to greet each other and grab a quick cup of coffee. I was in a hurry to take Lyla to her first of two medical visits required by the United States Embassy.

We arrived at Max Med, where the Embassy-approved doctor practiced. Dr. Bashaum was a very well-spoken man and was very easy to communicate with. We began our visit by showing him all of the medical records I had on Lyla. He was very interested in her heart procedure; he even asked what it cost.

I am often amused at how forward Indians can be, but they don't keep things as private as we do. He asked for various forms from the Embassy, one of which I did not have, giving me a moment of concern. He gave Lyla a quick check up and sent me upstairs to the nurses' station for her TB stick test to be done. The doctor told me to come back on Saturday, exactly 48 hours later, for the reading of her prick test. If clear, then we would go to the Embassy and do the visa interview on the next available day, which turned out to be Tuesday for us, because it was a holiday on Monday. He also told me I could

---

32 Name changed for security purposes.

bring the Embassy form I was missing, or I would have to pay $100 for the vaccines not on record.

I made a beeline for the Embassy. I was not about to lose $100 over a missing form!

The Embassy was not what I expected. I don't know why, but for some reason I pictured it as a replica of the Capitol building in D.C.. Nope, it was an Indian building with the American flag flying on it. I learned through the Facebook support groups that Americans are treated extra special there compared to nationals applying for travel visas. It was true. I was ushered right up to the front, but there was not much of a line anyway. I went inside and had the form within ten minutes. Later that afternoon, we got to know our new host family a little more. Lyla enjoyed playing with their children and in their neighborhood park.

The next morning, I awoke to the sound of pouring rain, such a soothing sound to me. Lyla and I did our normal morning routine and ate breakfast. We also played with play-dough for a while; it actually kept Lyla's attention for a long period of time, and that's a rarity. In addition, I got to exercise with my friend and relieve some stress.

Suddenly, Lyla got it in her mind that she was taking a bath. When I told her no, it was not bath time—Mayday! Mayday! Take cover! She threw one of her worst fits yet. She hit, bit, and pinched me. Phew, that was tough. If any of my kiddos at home did that, discipline would be swift and sure. I still struggled to find the right balance of love and discipline for Lyla. I could not isolate her because I did not want her to feel abandoned and, ultimately, she really wanted me there. I decided to separate her from me, but only by about an arm's length distance, just far enough that she could not reach me but close enough for her to know I was there.

During my time in India, I learned the way Indians say they are sorry is by grabbing both ear lobes. I motioned to her and told her she needed to tell me she was sorry. She knew exactly what I was telling her to do because she proceeded to ignore me. Then she held up one finger and blessed me out in Gujarati. Honestly, when she did that, I almost laughed out loud. She looked like a little adult trying to scold me. Of course, I didn't let her know how funny I thought her behavior was. I gave her a stern NO! Then she erupted into more screaming, more crying, and more drooling. I have never seen a child drool so much when they cry! She does it no matter how hard she cries. This also started to crack me up.

It was getting close to lunch time, so I told Lyla if she would calm down, we could go eat. She got quiet and walked to the door, but the moment I opened the door, she burst into tears and ran to my friend to be picked up and held. Thankfully, my friend knew how to respond and told Lyla she needed to go to her momma. Then Lyla cried more and returned to tell me off some more. This whole scenario repeated itself several times. After about 45 minutes of the tantrum, she smiled, grabbed her ears, and verbally said, "Sorry." I erupted into cheers and scooped her up, telling her how much I love to hold and hug her.

The next day we all piled into the Smiths' car and headed to Ambience Mall. Their oldest had a birthday party to attend there. They gave me a stroller to use, and Lyla and I did our own thing. Right after arriving at the mall, I received a huge blessing. My friends in Mumbai called and said they felt led to help me with my flight home. They said I should go ahead and book my flight in faith that I will get to leave late Tuesday/early Wednesday to head home, and if it did not work out, they would pay the change fee!

I was totally blown away by their generosity. It really helped in a lot of ways to go ahead and book the flight ahead of time: it gave us a lower ticket price, secured us a seat on a flight that might be full on a same-day booking, and did my heart good to know that home was just around the corner!

We had been blessed by our friends in India in many ways. Most of these friends I had never met until I arrived. In addition, there were some friends I never met but who assisted us online and, of course, the Russells, our friends in Jaipur, who prayed for us and gave us sound advice along the way. God was and is so faithful! This group of friends had blessed us spiritually with prayer and encouragement, fun fellowship, great shopping, and great advice. They helped us save money, found places for Lyla and I to stay, housed us, fed us, drove us around, washed our clothes, and now someone had offered to help pay for a flight change.

Again, we serve an AWESOME GOD who is FAITHFUL! To all my old and new friends in India: thank you for caring about us so much! You all became my church family there and helped meet all our needs. I will thank God for you in my prayers for many years to come!

Back at the mall, I was strolling Lyla around, and what do I see? A Starbucks. No need to ask if we stopped. I had a pumpkin spice latte, and Lyla had warm milk served to her in a Starbucks cup. She looked so cute drinking it like such a big girl.

Then we walked around and looked at a few stores and headed back to the Max Med Center for the reading of Lyla's TB test. I had been watching her arm where they pricked her, and there was no sign of a bump. I was pretty sure we were going to be in the clear!

At the doctor's office, I gave them the missing form from the Embassy. Soon they handed me my packet for the Embassy interview. It was a big, greenish sealed envelope that can be opened only by the Embassy. Receiving it meant we were cleared or else they wouldn't have given us the packet!

I continued to learn more valuable spiritual lessons throughout this process. The latest one had to do with distractions. I blogged:

> I am learning with Lyla that she does not have as many tantrums and break downs if I can minimize all of the chaos. Lots of times it helps if she and I can just be one-on-one. Now don't get me wrong . . . I am so thankful for everyone that has housed us, all their kiddos, and the activities, because they too have also helped Lyla. But she is most calm and seems more at peace when we are one-on-one.
>
> I was really thinking about this concept this week, and God showed me again . . . I am the same way. He desires to have one-on-one time with me. He knows it is beneficial to me. It brings me peace, it keeps me calm, it gives me security, and it gives me love.
>
> Too easily I get distracted by things that draw me away from time with Him, and my life soon becomes chaotic. I might even throw my own version of a tantrum.
>
> This has been a great reminder of how important one-on-one time with Him is in my life!
>
> This adoption process has been incredible. I am learning so much about myself and being challenged spiritually. I also think I will become a better parent to all of my children because of this experience.
>
> Lyla, thank you for making me a better Mom! I love you!

In addition to learning, I was growing in thankfulness and praise. Before we got Lyla, sometimes my heart would be sad thinking about her in an orphanage while we were all at home, doing things together. I thought about her being four and how I had missed certain milestones in her life.

Well, the reality was I had not missed much. There were so many things I was getting to experience with Lyla for the first time. I got to see her eyes light up and her little mind at work, just like my other kids when they saw something for the first time. In many ways, I taught her to walk, just like my other children. I heard her say her first English word and *Mommy* for the first time, just like my others. Because she is developmentally behind, I get to raise her up and teach her just like my other children.

I enjoyed spending my last bit of one-on-one time with Lyla during our last few days in New Delhi. We also enjoyed some fun outings to help pass the time. We went to church with the Smiths, we hung out with some dear friends from Jaipur, and we got the opportunity to share at an English Speaking School for Muslims.

This particular class was a discussion-based class; the students pick various topics and talk about them while working on their English and grammar. My friend thought our adoption would be a great discussion topic and also one that would open the door to some great spiritual discussion. And, it did! We talked back and forth for about an hour and a half, and God made a way for some super discussion. The students were so sweet to Lyla and really enjoyed having her there. Once again, I stood in awe as God used my four-year-old to plant seeds of the gospel!

After the class, we had an exciting adventure awaiting us. We went on a tour of the Toilet Museum! I think my most favorite part of this adventure was the drive over there. My friends from Jaipur joined us, and we were all in a taxi together. Our driver did not know exactly where he was going, and every time he pulled over and asked people where the toilet museum was, we all burst into laughter. I think we laughed harder in the car than in the museum. The museum was a little bit interesting, but kind of weird too. What can I say? It was a museum about toilets!

That evening I packed our bags in hopes that we would be headed home after our visa interview. I had already booked the flights.

We arrived early for our appointment at the Embassy. Immediately, I began to notice things were not right. At the first desk, I was asked why I had that appointment form and not one for adoption, but he gave me a number and ushered me down to the visa office. At this point, I felt great about being an American. There was a huge line of Indians waiting, and I was ushered past them, right over to an area by myself where I had little wait at all. I almost burst into Lee Greenwood's song, "I'm Proud to be an American," right then and there. But I contained myself and felt thankful this was one place in India where I had a little control.

But, apparently not as much control as I thought. When called to the window, I learned I should have had a different appointment set up, one that should have been set before I ever came to India. Unfortunately, I had not been given a lot of information about my travels, what to expect, and what documents were needed. My trip to get Lyla was a little unconventional, since we got her before we had her passport.

As the lady at the window told me I did not have the correct appointment and acted like she was going to send me away, I lost all control. I burst into deep sobs, and tears started pouring out. I did not drool like Lyla does when she cries, but I started crying so hard I could not talk. Another lady ran to the window and said, "Control yourself, madam!"

Once I could finally talk, I explained my situation. "We have been here for a month. No one informed me there should have been a preset interview. We had delays with my daughter's passport. We were delayed so long my husband had to go back, and I have been here two weeks alone. I have children at home, and my husband needs me. I have a flight booked tonight, and I need my daughter's visa!" More tears . . .

The ladies discussed it among themselves. The lady behind the desk asked if I had everything I needed for the interview and the medical packet. When I said yes, they agreed to help me. Hallelujah! I set Lyla down with some play-dough and was prepared to stay as long as was needed to get the visa in hand!

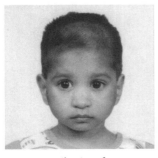

Ami's visa photo

I went through all the necessary paperwork and had a short interview with an officer. He mainly asked questions about our adoption experience, and I kept my answers brief. He then said they would do everything possible to get me my visa today, but because my interview was impromptu, there were some things they still needed to clear. That meant I would have to wait until Thursday to get it because of the holiday on Wednesday. I almost cried again, but the officer said, "Please don't cry, madam. We will try very hard."

"I am staying in the area for lunch and will wait on your call," I replied.

Lyla and I headed to lunch at the swanky Leelah's Palace. I had resigned myself to the thought we were not going to get the visa today. I tried to enjoy my lunch and get my mind wrapped around the fact Lyla and I were going to be here another two days.

And then I received a call. "Madam, your visa is ready for pickup."

Lyla and I did the happy dance all the way back to the Embassy. It was a quick pick up, and off we went to say our good-byes to the Smith family, pick up our luggage, and leave on a jet plane. India, you were good to us, but we were ready to go home!

Chapter 13

HOME

LYLA AND I MADE THE 22-hour flight home successfully. We landed in Atlanta and had to go through Customs and Immigration before we could see our family, who were as anxious to see us as I was to see them. I had been gone for almost five weeks!

Scott and I wondered how Lyla would react to seeing him again; it had been two weeks since he had left us behind in India.

Lyla and I met with a border control agent. After a brief interview and a review of our paperwork, the agent informed me, "Your daughter will become a United States citizen at midnight tonight." Then she extended her hand and said, "Congratulations and welcome to the United States of America."

Wow! Those were some incredible words to hear. I almost broke into tears again, recalling how far we had come. Especially how far Lyla had come—starting in a little village outside of Ahmedabad, being shuffled to two orphanages, being chosen at the age of two, meeting her new parents two years later, having heart surgery, going through recovery, seeing and experiencing India for a little while, and now becoming a United States citizen!

But there was no time for tears. We quickly gathered our luggage and tried to get out of the customs area to see our family. When we first walked out, I could not find anyone. Then I saw Scott waving his hands frantically, and we ran toward him. Seth and Levi dashed toward me. We hugged tightly—I did not want to let them go! Katy Pierce ran as fast as her little legs would let her, and when Joel was placed in my arms, he looked at me for a few seconds, and then his face broke into a huge smile; he did remember me after my five-week absence. Lyla flew from my side and ran to Scott when she spotted him; she grabbed Scott immediately and clung to him. It was a good sign she was attached to him.

I looked around at our little homecoming and realized again how blessed we were. Others had come to wait for our arrival: several friends from our church in Tennessee, my parents from South Carolina, Scott's mom from Mississippi, and Amanda Carroll from several hours away came to welcome us home too. Everyone met Lyla, we took pictures and chatted, and we all rejoiced together. It was a happy, happy day.

We left the airport and ate a good American meal at Chick-fil-A. Life was good! We drove home to Tennessee, eager to show Lyla her

Meeting at the airport—together at last!

new home and the bedroom she would share with Katy Pierce. We had decorated their room with handmade Indian bedcoverings, curtains, and pictures to welcome her. Life felt complete!

"And they lived happily ever after."

Not! I would like to interject a warning to families considering adoption. I think many hopeful adoptive parents, including myself, often see adoption with a fairytale ending, but this is not reality. Adoption is tough and certainly not for the faint of heart, but I believe it's that way to shape us and to allow God to get the glory. It is a physical, emotional, spiritual, and relational struggle to incorporate a "stranger," although the adoption certificate says it's your child, into your home. There are tantrums from both the adopted child and the biological children (and maybe even the parents). There are changes and adjustments to make in all family members' routines and in the overall household management. There are hidden problems that can surface once home, and there may be additional unforeseen financial costs.

As if child-rearing wasn't hard enough in itself, adoption adds tension to discovering the right balance when disciplining the new child, who is still adjusting, and trying to discipline the siblings fairly. I have mentioned several times our family struggled to find the balance of being sensitive to Lyla's background and her personal issues, yet tried not to treat her differently from our other children. It can—no, it *does*—add extra strain and stress on a family.

When a family adopts, they accept a child or teen who potentially carries a whole bunch of "baggage," and they integrate that child into a family with its own set of imperfections. Families have to work hard to wade through all of the junk and persevere to the end to finish strong. However, it's amazing how God takes so many blemished, imperfect families and uses them for His glory. It is a beautiful picture of redemption.

Our family was no different. Although she was now ours, we were working and adjusting to our new normal, our forever family. I had a phone conversation with a friend a few days after we arrived home. I explained all of us were having some adjustment aches and pains here and there, and she said something I had not considered. She asked, "Do you realize your family has gone from having two children to five children in only 18 months?" The thought had never crossed my mind! My family had been adjusting for 18 months as we had added three new members.

Overall, Scott and I knew it wouldn't be easy. We were generally pleased with the progress in our family bonding and everyone's transition into being a member of a family of seven. There were definitely struggles, but I could not have been more proud of my two oldest, Seth and Levi.

I think they were a little let down on their very first time meeting Lyla. I believe they expected her to be as excited to meet them that day at the airport, but she had eyes only for Scott. The first few days at home with us, she still acted a little scared and shy and remained glued to Scott and me. They pointed out that she sure was getting a lot of attention.

We had a long talk about how special they are and how much they mean to us. We explained, "God has used this whole adoption process to grow us and stretch us as parents, and now God is using it to grow and stretch you." This was a time when they needed to think more about their new sister than themselves, and it might be that way for a while as she adjusted to having a family of her own. They accepted what we said and acted as awesome big brothers do. They were patient with her and with us, and they loved and doted on her and even played with her a good bit. They tried to teach her English words for their toys, and they were proud to introduce her to their friends. I think the adoption had not only made Scott and me better parents, but her brothers and sister were becoming better siblings too!

My little Katy Pierce struggled a bit. In the beginning, Katy Pierce was jealous of Lyla hanging onto her daddy; at the airport when Scott held both of them in his arms for a picture, Katy Pierce sneaked a quick "punch" in to let Lyla know she didn't like it. The first few days after we were home, she didn't want Lyla to touch her toys at times. She would point her tiny finger at Lyla and holler out, "No no, Wywa!" Lyla would not be upset but would try to avoid Katy Pierce after that. Katy Pierce was certainly being territorial.

We realized that behavior may not have been an adoption adjustment issue as much as it was simply a normal reaction for a toddler. Katy Pierce was only 18 months at the time, and she wasn't accustomed to sharing her toys; her brothers hadn't been interested in her dolls and girl toys.

As a few days went by, the girls soon began to play together and bond. Soon Katy Pierce and Lyla were laughing and giggling, chasing each other around the house, and taking turns being the chaser. In addition, Lyla's presence helped us solve a nap and bedtime problem we had been working on with Katy Pierce. Before Lyla came, Katy Pierce would scream and cry herself to sleep when we laid her down in her crib for naps or at night. But now, she went right to sleep because her sister, Lyla, was in the room with her.

The baby of the family, Joel, well, he was just along for the ride of this new transition. He thought Lyla was hilarious. He laughed all of the time, even if she just crossed the room. Lyla was very affectionate with him and often tried to help bottle feed him and tickle him. He laughed out loud every time she was around and gave her his award-winning grin! He adored his new sister. And Lyla adored him. When Joel dropped a toy or his blanket, she would jump up and run to take care of him. If I was in another room and Joel would cry, Lyla would race to find me. She would tug on my clothes and speak excitedly with her Indian jibber-jabber, wanting me to hurry to Joel.

I wasn't only worried about how my biological kids were adjusting, I was also worried about Lyla. Our boys could voice their concerns or feelings, but we could only guess at what Lyla was thinking or feeling. One day, Rupa, our Indian friend in Manchester, came to meet Lyla. Rupa speaks Gujarati and Hindi and tried to communicate with Lyla in both Gujarati and Hindi, but Lyla was not very responsive in either language. We wondered if Lyla feared that Rupa was there to take her away since she was Indian. Lyla finally spoke a little to Rupa, and Rupa told me she was conversing in Hindi, but not a word in Gujarati. This surprised me since that was the language used by the caregivers at the orphanage. But Rupa made my day when she translated something Lyla said in Hindi. Lyla pointed to Joel and told Rupa, "Joel is my baby brother."

That statement relieved my fears about how Lyla was feeling. While I had some slight nagging concerns about Lyla not communicating very much in any language, I thought her comment about Joel was sweet. It assured my heart that she had accepted us as her family.

Lyla was fitting in and adjusting pretty well. There were certain things about her that I noticed, such as her need for constant affirmation. We were all willing to encourage her, but when I say constant, I mean *constant*! For example, when eating, every time she took a bite, she wanted me to clap for her. When I would grow weary of cheering on every little bite, I reminded myself that, unlike my other children, she had never had anyone to cheer for her and clap for her in all the little things she did.

Also, Lyla was not good at sitting still. She was in constant motion. I wasn't sure if she was simply curious and over-stimulated with all the material things we have in our house compared to her sterile environment in the orphanage, or if she simply had tons of energy. She hardly ever watched television. Occasionally she would sit and watch something for about five minutes, but then she was off and exploring again. She was constantly underfoot, checking out everything each of us was doing.

Her eating was developing slowly. I felt like she was on a roll with it in India, and then her progression seemed to slow down when we got back home. It took me quite a while to get her to eat a slice of bread or a sandwich. Shortly after she had been home, she and I had a major blowout over food, but it was really more about her wanting to be in control. Our showdown took place over lunch, and it lasted a few hours. Lyla was definitely strong-willed, but so am I, and I let her know Momma was going to win!

Again, I was still navigating my way through the proper time and way to discipline her or whether to ignore her tantrums. I wanted her to eat because she was so tiny. At the age of four, she weighed less than Katy Pierce at 18 months and Joel, a little chunky monkey, was only two pounds lighter than Lyla!

Because of spending so much time with doctors in India, when we got back to the States I decided to give Lyla a little break before we rushed her back to see doctors again. Overall, her health seemed to be on a steady incline. She continued to take her heart medicine and displayed no issues from her surgical procedure. But Scott and I worried since she didn't eat much and seemed so tiny, so we scheduled some appointments with our family pediatrician and with the International Adoption Clinic at Vanderbilt. After our first appointment with the International Adoption Clinic at Vanderbilt, we learned Lyla had a parasite, giardia, common to third world countries in her digestive system. This parasite was keeping her from getting the much-needed nutrients she needed to continue her growth and development. She received prescriptions to help her fight this parasite. What a relief to see her overall health improve once we rid her body of giardia.

We also learned from her x-rays that Lyla had suffered a severe skull fracture as an infant. The doctors located this information in the medical files we were given at the orphanage. We had been completely unaware. We would continue to follow up on how this fracture might affect her as she grew older.

On the positive side, even though we continued to struggle with her at mealtime, I was delighted to see how strong-willed she was becoming. That sounds hard to believe, doesn't it, that a parent would take delight in a child's strong will? I believe being strong-willed is a strength that can be channeled in a great way to do great things as she grows older! She displayed confidence and boldness as well. I anticipated bringing home a timid, meek child, but she was demanding and pushy—confident! I am glad she felt comfortable in our home to be herself and to express her personality.

She was learning to express herself in words as well. She was mimicking much less and saying a few words on her own. In India, we developed the habit of using our hands and motions to communicate with her, but now we worked hard to force her to talk without motions. The boys were a big help, patiently repeating words for her to say. She had learned the names of her siblings quickly and often called out to "Sef," "Wee-bi," "K-pwis," and "Jol."

During the aches and pains of adjustment, God continued to bless us. It was not long after we came home, our health insurance agent contacted us to say they would reimburse us for her surgery after all! We were so appreciative and excited to be reimbursed; we took that unexpected money and sent it as a donation for Chadasha, knowing the money would be put to good use by Dr. Dorion.

I think it is noteworthy to share this amazing story, which affirms more of God's provisions: Scott had anticipated there would be some extra general expenses here and there once we were in India, such as transportation or food, and he set aside some money to use if needed. It was wise he did, because there were several things that came up during our stay. He had determined we probably would be in debt for about $1,000 when we all returned to the States. When he arrived home, he sat down to complete an accounting of our money and balance the budget and determine our personal debt. He calculated the total amount we had received from generous donations, fundraisers, and from our Scentsy sales, and then he calculated all the expenses we had documented. Incredibly, it was **an even match**. Every need had been covered, and we were not even one cent in debt. Thank You, Lord, for your promises and Your provisions!

Concerned with finding ways to encourage bonding in our family, I spoke with other adoptive families to get advice. One suggestion was to stay at home as much as possible in the beginning, to spend quality time together as a nuclear family. They recommended avoiding having extended family or friends holding, feeding, or giving gifts to the adopted child. Taking these precautions would help to prevent the child from developing indiscriminate affection. In other words, if given love by everyone, the child would not feel bonded to one particular unit but would go to anyone. We would need to avoid excessive interactions, which could interfere or delay the tight family connection we were working to build.

Following this advice, we tried to spend the majority of our time at home. About the only people we exposed her to were those at church and in restaurants. It was at church where I understood why others recommended not allowing other people to pick her up. At first, it overwhelmed her; she would pull away, not wanting people to come and grab her for a hug. If she wanted to hug, she wanted to initiate it. However, once she learned church was a comfortable, secure place, she soaked in all the attention she could get, and trust me, everyone at church lavished it on her. She was constantly held and passed around.

Again, it was not because we didn't want others to love on her or enjoy her. After all, they had journeyed with us and rejoiced and suffered alongside of us in every twist and turn. Many of them had been our cheerleaders, our counselors, our comforters, and our prayer warriors! They played a huge part in Lyla being here, and we couldn't have finished the process without them! But there were two potential problems creeping up: Lyla needed to practice her walking, and she was exhibiting signs of indiscriminate affection.

As for her walking, she needed to continue to build stamina and strength in her legs. She was absolutely dainty, cute, and irresistible, but all the holding of her made it difficult to encourage her development and force her to walk. Every time I turned around, she was in someone's arms. Everyone loved holding her, and she loved being held and babied, but that wouldn't help her get stronger.

The second problem involved her displaying indiscriminate affection. Church was one major love-fest for her. She ran to anyone and everyone for attention and affection. Lyla knew exactly what she was doing. She knew she could misbehave at church and not get in trouble, since I would not discipline her as strongly in public as I would at home. If we did scold her at church, others would come to her defense. In fact, she had many women wrapped around her finger from church, women who already loved her like she was one of their own grandchildren.

I recall how Lyla pulled at the heartstrings of two women in particular, Vickie and Donna. While they never undermined our discipline of Lyla, they would let us know in a jovial way that they did not like to see "their girl" upset. One morning as the service started, I got onto Lyla for misbehaving, and Lyla buried her face in her hands and started crying. I glanced up and felt the piercing eyes of Donna from the choir loft, letting me know she didn't appreciate me hurting her girl's feelings. I almost laughed out loud, as Donna was teasing me but getting her point across too. There were other funny times when a crying Lyla would run and throw herself into Vickie's lap. And while Lyla wasn't looking, Vickie would give us a stern look and ask, "What have you done to my girl?"

Our church family adored Lyla, and she knew it! She was loved and protected, and she manipulated the situation in her favor for sure. However, we still needed to fix her issue of showing indiscriminate affection. Scott and I decided to write a letter to our church family on Facebook to help us with this predicament.

Trinity Friends,

We need your help with something concerning our daughter, Lyla. We are trying to teach her appropriate behavior in social settings and how to have proper boundaries and social skills with friends and strangers. Since we have brought her from India, she quickly runs to people she does not know, or does not know well, and asks to be held. Part of this is that she never really bonded with any adult before she was placed in our family. In order to help her to properly bond to us, as parents, and to teach her how to properly relate to friends and strangers, we are asking everyone to please not pick her up and hold her. Even if she runs to you in the hall or if you are with her in the nursery. Please feel free to give her a high five, or shake her hand, or bend down and greet her with a little side hug.

Thanks for your help. While Kelly and I, and the rest of our children, know that you guys are safe and our friends, Lyla is unable to determine who is a friend and who is a stranger at this point. Right now, we need her to learn that her family are the only ones who can have that closeness with her. In time, she will know and learn how much our church is like family too! Thanks again!

~ Scott and Kelly

Our church rallied behind us and helped us properly teach Lyla about boundaries in social settings. However, I started to feel sorry for my biological children. Lyla was the center of attention everywhere we went. In fact, let me be transparent in sharing this story:

During the adoption process, I found myself at times getting defensive for Lyla. I feared that our friends and family wouldn't love her as much as our other children because she was adopted. I had built up these scenarios in my mind, in which I would love and console her through her rejection. But when she got here, I found it to be just the opposite. Lyla was the center of attention. And I know it was not purposeful; well-meaning friends and family wanted to express full acceptance of Lyla into our family. But there were times I felt our biological children were being ignored. I found myself getting very protective of them and starting to resent Lyla. Of course, I didn't show her my resentment because deep down I understood that she wasn't responsible for what was happening. But I could feel the bond I had developed with her lessening.

I confessed it to Scott and shared my personal struggle with other adoptive families to seek their input. My friends encouraged me to do small things with Lyla to re-strengthen our bond, like hold her and look into her eyes while she was drinking her milk, almost like bottle-feeding a baby. But my friends also encouraged me to continue to protect my biological children. They thought I was doing what was crucial and beneficial for them as well. Scott and I concluded that he would pour more of himself into Lyla so she could get her needs met, and I could pour myself into our biological children so they could get their needs met.

It took me a few months to rebuild my maternal bond with Lyla. I don't think she ever knew I was struggling, but I knew it and felt like a horrible mother. God was showing me it was a heart issue of mine, and yet this process was revealing all the ugliness of sin I had within me. But through God's grace, Scott's encouragement, and my prayers, I worked through it.

I don't know that my other four children were really struggling with resentment, but I did sense an occasional feeling of rejection in them. For the most part, I could see they were handling it well. I was excited when someone from church brought us a meal one night and included a gift. She told me it was for all of the children. When I told the kids they had a present, Seth said, "It's probably for Lyla." When they learned it was for all of them, they all got excited. It was nice of this friend to bless all of them.

But, in everyone's defense, I understood the buzz about Lyla. It was kind of like having a newborn. Our biological children, of course, could not remember the fanfare and parties thrown in their honor when they were born. So, we shared those memories with them as well.

Lyla wasn't home two weeks before she had participated in all kinds of new activities. She had her first swimming experience when our church hosted a big indoor swim party at our community recreation center. She thoroughly enjoyed the swimming pool. I figured she would, as much as she loved baths! She had a ball splashing around and playing with her daddy.

She also celebrated Halloween for the first time, dressed in costume as an Indian princess. Sweet little Grace from Ahmedabad had given her a precious pink sari as a hand-me-down. When Lyla put it on, she sashayed all over the house with the pallu (the piece that goes over your shoulder like a throw) held ever so elegantly by her hand and shoulder. It was so precious! We carved pumpkins and took her on her first trick-or-treat extravaganza. She received each piece of candy with pure joy and enthusiasm.

After being with us a little over six weeks, Lyla said something magnificent. My little girl rounded the corner from the kitchen to the living room. She came to me with her lips puckered out as far as they could go. She kissed me, and then in her precious broken English, she said, "I lud choo."

I took a deep breath, fighting back the tears.

I was already emotional because earlier that day I had been re-living our adoption journey in my mind; November is *Adoption Awareness Month* and that particular day was Orphan Sunday in many churches across America. Many heartfelt memories came to mind. I concluded, *I am so blessed! I can't believe I get to be her mother. To think, my little girl who had not even put a sentence together yet and could barely speak English, told me the most wonderful words a mother could hear: "I love you!"*

I recalled an incredible song, "Orphan," written by Ronnie Freeman. This song held significant meaning for me during the adoption. I first heard it sung in church one Easter. I quickly put together a video compilation* of our adoption story with Lyla, using this song as the background music, and posted it online.

You think so much of me
You take delight in me
You paid the price for me
Then you adopted me

I'm not an orphan anymore, I'm yours
I stand before you now adored, I'm yours
Your cross has set me free
New life belongs to me
I'm not an orphan anymore I'm yours

You took my guilt and shame
Gave me a brand new name
You call me your beloved
I call you Abba father

I'm not an orphan anymore, I'm yours
I stand before you now adored, I'm yours
Your cross has set me free
New life belongs to me
I'm not an orphan anymore, I'm yours

* http://heknowshername.blogspot.com/2013_11_01_archive.html.

Now I feast at the table of the King
And His love is the banner over me
His love is the banner over me,
the banner over me, the banner over me.[33]

I considered all the Lord had done for me personally: He saved me, gave me an incredible life, and cast a banner of love over me. I was broken to think He had done all of this for me, for my family, and especially for little Lyla Ruth. I was and am still in awe of a God who literally brought people together from our city, our state, our country, and the world to participate in our adoption. Truly, each and every person was an integral part of this exceptional journey! And all along, He was and is the Master Author writing this incredible story.

In the song, *Orphan*, the final two words in the chorus, "I'm yours"[34] speak loudly to me. These two words bring to mind the spiritual transformation that occurred in our own extraordinary adoption story. From the beginning of our adoption process, a verse in Isaiah had been essential to us. In this verse, the Lord declares, "I have called you by name, you are mine" (Is. 43:1b, ESV). We had responded back to our Lord with a resounding "I'm yours," and because we did, we will never be the same.

And they lived radically changed ever after . . .

---

33 Ronnie Freeman, "Not an Orphan," *ronnie freeman* (blog), Jan 5, 2012, http://blog.ronniefreemanonline.com/?p=73.
34 Ibid., accessed July 5, 2015.

Chapter 14

TWO YEARS LATER . . .

LYLA RUTH HAS BEEN WITH us almost two years now. Our family is thriving and doing well. I almost feel guilty sometimes about how smooth our transition has been. I read horror stories and chat with other adoptive parents who have faced some really tough issues with their adoptive and biological children during their transition phase. Has our transition been perfect? No way, because we are human and full of problems. But truly our transition into becoming an interracial, large adopting family has been wonderful. The tough parts have grown us spiritually, and for that we are thankful!

I want to start with her health. Her heart condition is completely repaired. We still praise God and thank Him for Babyheart and Dr. Clint Dorion in Knoxville, Tennessee, for their help in acquiring a surgeon for Lyla and helping us financially. We keep in touch with them periodically to let them know of our great appreciation and to update them on Lyla's continued progress. We also connect with Dr. Suman and Dr. Gopi in Hyderabad from time to time to thank them again and let them see how well "the People's Girl" is doing.

Thanks to the discovery of the parasite and getting it out of her system and to her successful heart surgery, Lyla has come a long way. She is still pretty tiny and petite for a six-year-old, but she has put on some weight and has grown about five inches these past two years. I think she will always be my dainty Indian princess.

As to her issue with the fractured skull, we have recurring visits with the clinic to continue to monitor her growth and some of the developmental delays she has exhibited in coordination, speech, and language.

Speaking of developmental delays, these have carried on into her academics. She is behind in school, as was expected. She did not grow up in a nurturing environment that stimulated her brain growth, and she is still learning English. While her communication skills have come light years beyond what they used to be, her evaluations conclude she is developmentally delayed compared to the average six-year-old.

Lyla was able to start preschool a few months after being home. She was in the same class as Levi, and he helped watch out for her. We were blessed with such an incredible preschool teacher, Cathy Hand, who goes to our church. We saw so much growth and improvement in Lyla due to having that structured environment and wonderful peer models around her.

She has an Individualized Education Plan (IEP) to assist her learning team in making appropriate educational decisions for her. As part of her team, we were glad it was recommended for her to repeat preschool another school year. She was receiving physical therapy as part of her schooling, but she progressed enough physically that she met the goals set for her. Her physical development remains a work-in-progress, but she recently and proudly learned to pedal a bike with training wheels; this was a huge milestone for her. She still receives occupational therapy because she is lacking in some fine motor skills. At the writing of this book, she struggles to write her name. However, this child blows me away with how far she has come in such a short time. It may take a few years, but we have hope one day she will be able to catch up to her age and peer group. But, if she doesn't, we are okay with that too.

Lyla's personality is still so bubbly, enthusiastic, silly, and giddy. She is rarely in a bad mood, and if she is in a mood, it usually doesn't last long. One of my most favorite things to do with her is pick out her clothes each day. Her reaction is priceless. She thinks every out-fit is fantastic, and the shinier the better! She finds joy in the little things we take for granted. Literally, as we gather her clothes each day, she squeals in excitement, gasps for air, and claps her hands. Early on, she would say, "Mine, Lyla," pointing to herself. Now she says, "Oh, Mom, I love it!" And if the outfit is extra girly and shiny, the reaction is intensified!

She also shows this same ecstatic reaction when she is picked up from school every afternoon. EVERY afternoon, no exaggeration, and especially if it is her daddy getting her. She squeals with delight, smiling and jumping up and down in excitement as if she has not seen us in weeks. Her contagious smile and bright attitude earned her the Bubblegum Award—for always having a bubbly spirit and happy attitude—this past year in Preschool. Everyone in her elementary school adores her. It's hard not to love someone who is always happy and eager to learn.

Another favorite memory in the past two years was seeing Lyla celebrate Christmas for the first time. She could not get over all the presents and decorations. Before she opened every present, she laughed, clapped, and jumped up and down. After opening each present, she then walked around to each family member and announced, "Lyla, mine," as she pointed to each present. She did this so much, and kept going on and on about it, that Katy Pierce, then 20 months old, exclaimed loudly, "Hush, Wywa!" Needless to say, Lyla was ecstatic about Christmas and opening presents.

Lyla's fifth birthday

I don't know who had more fun celebrating her first birthday with us, Lyla or me. During the time we waited to adopt, I regretted missing her birthdays. We had celebrated two of them without her. So we did it big for our first one together and her 5th birthday! We used the fellowship hall at the church and decorated the entire room with tulle and rose petals. We had tiaras and party hats and balloons, and we displayed her pictures from our referral along with a new portrait. We had a big sign that read, "Happily ever after starts here!" She was a princess for the day, wearing a purple pageant dress, and dear friends helped make it a special party. In addition, among the guests were Ajay and Smita Carroll and Indian children from some other adoptive families. It was a noteworthy day in my book to finally celebrate with my girl!

During the past two years, there were so many other firsts we shared with her. Each and every holiday, such as Thanksgiving, Valentine's Day, Easter, and Independence Day, brought new experiences. Even the changes in the weather—snow, spring flowers, and fall breezes—were all so new to her. We took her to the beach for the first time, to her first Clemson football game, and to her first county fair. We enjoyed watching her as she soaked it all in.

Lyla Ruth Ami Parkison

Lyla Ruth Ami Parkison amazes me every day. Throughout our journey, people told me how much Lyla would be blessed to be a part of our family. Well, we are the blessed ones! I love you, Lyla Ruth! Thank you for making me a better follower of Jesus and a better mother. Never forget God chose you, and Daddy and Momma chose you!

"I have called you by name, you are mine!"

~ Isaiah 43:1b, ESV

Chapter 15

RISE UP AND BUILD . . . THE STORY CONTINUES

DURING THE LONG, GRUELING PROCESS of adopting Lyla, God began calling me again to something I never expected.

Our family had been matched with Lyla for about three months, and Katy Pierce was a tiny little newborn. I was hosting a women's Bible study in my home the summer of 2012. We were studying Kelly Minter's Bible study book, *Nehemiah: A Heart That Can Break*. "Nehemiah had to have a heart that could break so he could restore a wall that was broken. In this 7-session Bible study for women, Nehemiah's heart for the oppressed, suffering, and poor is a beacon whose light shines on the current call of the church to be the hands and feet of Jesus."

This study was right up my alley. I love missions and studying anything about missions, but I didn't know I would be personally challenged. In the book, Kelly Minter often asked the question, "So for what purpose is God breaking your heart?"[35]

---

35 Kelly Minter, "Bible Studies," *Kelly Minter: Author, speaker, and musician*, 2014, https://kellyminter.com/store/.

When I first saw that question, I anxiously responded, "Lord, don't burden my heart for anything else. I have enough going on as it is." I quickly tallied up all the things I was doing for the Lord in my mind and thought to myself, *my heart can't be broken anymore; I have nothing else left to give.*

As the study went on, I knew the Lord was not satisfied with my answer. I could feel Him drawing me back to that same question again and again. Finally, I gave in. I prayed, "Lord, what cause or whom do you want me to be broken for?" The Lord spoke. I don't know how to describe His voice. The Lord speaks to me all the time through the Word, worship, prayer, and through people, but there are three times in my life when, without a shadow of doubt, I heard the Lord speak in a unique way to me. This was the third time.

When it has occurred, I didn't hear a loud, booming voice; it's more like a soft voice bringing clarity and peace. It's like I hear the message clearly at the same time I see it in my head and feel the Holy Spirit moving in my soul. This is the message I heard, saw, and felt: "I don't want your family to only adopt an orphan, but I want your family to do more." It was clear to me the message was from the Lord and it had something to do with orphans. But the "more" part of the message was still unknown to me.

I immediately became overwhelmed with fear and inadequacy. I found this difficult to share with anyone but Scott since the task God wanted me to do was uncertain. Even though I was unsure where the Lord was leading me, I knew He was calling me to do something so much bigger than myself, and He was leading my family to join with me in support. It was exciting, yet scary and humbling.

Because everything remained vague, I began brainstorming all of the things it could be. Maybe I was supposed to become an adoption agent or a social worker to perform home study reports. I jumped online and started looking into getting a Masters in social work, but then abruptly stopped.

I did something truly against my nature. I decided to pray and wait. Scott and I prayed about this for almost two years and waited for an answer, which went even more against my impatient nature. I prayed, "Lord, with what cause are You burdening me and leading me to undertake?" During those two years, God would reveal little snippets or insights to lead me to the answer.

Here are some of my insights: First, my heart was becoming more broken for India. Images and stories from visiting so many orphanages, including Lyla's, constantly came to mind. I was hearing more about the horrors of sex trafficking victims. Reading stories about widows who are thrown out on the streets, considered cursed when their husbands passed away, filled me with sorrow. I became even more burdened when contemplating the vast numbers of lost people all over South Asia and the unreached people groups of India. I could not forget learning that India is one of the leading countries in the world with the largest numbers of orphans and sex trafficking victims.[36]

Second, I became more broken for the needy children and the growing number of sex trafficking victims in my own country. I felt God was leading me to do something in both India and at home in America.

---

36 Narayan Lakshman, "India among worst ranked countries in tackling human trafficking," *The Hindu*, June 16, 2010, accessed July 6, 2015, http://www. thehindu.com/news/india-among-worst-ranked-countries-in-tackling-human-trafficking/article4584420.ece.

In addition, the Lord made several other things clear to me. He did not mean my family was supposed to pack up and move to India to be missionaries. Neither was I supposed to allow these new burdens on my heart to take away from my primary calling as a wife, mother of five, and pastor's wife. Furthermore, this new vision should not interfere with my husband's ministry in the local church, as Scott and I still possessed a deep desire to serve in the local church and within our own community. My hope was this summons from the Lord would only augment the church and its ministries. I knew in some way He was calling me to minister to orphans, sexually abused women, widows, and the lost, which goes right along with the mission of the church.

Indian Mommas

On March 2, 2014, a little less than two years from my initial call from God, I took a Mom's get-away weekend with three other moms who are adoptive parents of children from India. We spent the weekend relaxing and laughing and discussing what God was doing in our lives and families. We also shared special prayer requests.

I had purposely not taken a turn and spoken up about what God was doing in my life; I wanted to catch up on all He was doing in my friends' lives first and didn't want to miss any of their stories. Besides, I had planned on leaving early to make it back to church to hear some IMB missionaries speak on Sunday, and I wanted to hear about my friends before I left. We talked late into the day, and something nagged at me to stay over. We went to breakfast that Sunday morning, and at the restaurant my friends reminded me I had not taken time to share. I hesitated at first. I had not spoken about this call with others, but I went for it. I blurted out, "I believe God is calling me to build an orphanage and a women's shelter for sex trafficking victims, and widows in India and possibly even here in the United States."

My friends were ecstatic, overjoyed, and filled with excitement and began to throw ideas back and forth. They started making plans to rally their churches to support the cause. Their excitement and reaction to jump on board was affirmation to me that I had correctly interpreted the Lord's calling, and their support fueled the fire of my new passion.

At the same time we were discussing my call, my church was having the service in which the IMB missionaries were guest speakers. I was sorry to miss it, but I trusted it was a powerful service. My husband confirmed how great it was when I returned home. And powerful it was! The next morning, I received a phone call from a young woman at church. I could tell by her tone she was hesitant and nervous to talk to me. She finally admitted, "During the service yesterday, I felt the Lord speak to me. I don't know why, but He clearly said for me to sell everything I own and move to India to help Kelly."

I was dumbfounded, and so was she, but both for different reasons. I was blown away because God had just ignited a huge spark in me the day before when He confirmed my call through my friends, and simultaneously, He was backing it up by calling someone at my church to be involved! My friend was even more amazed as I relayed to her the call God had placed in my heart. No one had any knowledge about this new ministry I was called to start, and God revealed it to her Himself. Again, it was another affirmation that we were hearing accurately, and I watched as God began raising up others to help me.

Soon after these confirmations, I established a 501(c)3 nonprofit in order to collect funding to start these building projects. With the help of a friend, I named it *LOFT 218: Rise Up and Build*. *LOFT* is an acronym for Least OF These, and 218 comes from Nehemiah 2:18; in this chapter and verse, a group of people were inspired to "Rise Up and Build" and serve a group of people in need. Again, this was from the book I studied when I felt called to start this ministry.

There are three principles God has made clear for *LOFT 218*: Our first principle, the heartbeat of our ministry, is that the **Gospel** and church planting are to be our number one priority. While all the humanitarian efforts and projects we will be doing will be valuable and life-changing for those involved, we can never elevate the humanitarian aspect of this ministry over the power of the gospel. There is nothing that will make a greater difference in the lives of the oppressed than Jesus Christ Himself. This is why our number one strategy for LOFT 218 is to plant our ministry in the geographical area of an unreached, unengaged people group to make a deeper impact for His kingdom.

Our second principle is **Generosity**. God has already been pouring out His abundant blessings and provisions on our ministry. We will be generous in return and desire to give ten percent of our funds to help other ministries and to partner with them in Kingdom work.

The third principle is **Going**. We desire to partner with churches and organizations by encouraging, facilitating, and/or leading teams to be on mission for God. With our Indian partners in place, we can help short-term mission teams maximize their gifts by providing them with a missions experience with both gospel and humanitarian focuses.

Since those confirmations from God, God has continued to affirm and direct me in this calling. One way He has confirmed everything is through His provision. Friends, even strangers, have heard about *LOFT 218* and have given generously. In addition, we have started selling fair trade items from India to raise money as well. A woman in South Carolina who was closing her bridal shop even donated most of her unsold dresses to be sold for *LOFT*. Our website, www.loft218.org, provides information about ways to assist. Even the sale of this book is helping *LOFT 218*! (Thanks to you, the readers!)

In addition to finances, God has provided church partners. Other churches in Georgia, Tennessee, and South Carolina are interested in partnering with us to accomplish the **Gospel, Generosity, and Going** principles and joining us to see *LOFT 218* come to fruition.

While there are still some unknowns regarding exactly how everything is going to be done and when it is going to be completed, God has revealed each piece in His perfect time, which has given me the freedom not to worry about it. When He reveals something to do, I move forward; when He holds back, I hold back too, and I sit and wait on Him. In this manner, He gets all of the glory, and no one can take credit from Him or boast in their own works.

Recently, I traveled with a team from my church to India and visited a piece of land in Rajasthan. We prayed over the land and feel strongly this is where the orphanage should be located. Now we wait with great expectation to see how the Lord will provide the finances. At this moment, I am still waiting for doors to open to start an orphanage for children in the United States as well. I know God will provide people who will *Rise Up and Build*!

One can only imagine the difficulty in trying to accomplish a task such as this in a foreign country while living half a world away, but God has taken care of all

With the land for LOFT 218

these details. We now have partners in India who are joining with us. In fact, God had already given a vision to one of our partners two years prior to go ahead and legally establish a nonprofit society in Rajasthan. Amazingly, it even included a clause for an orphanage and a shelter. God had already navigated it all so *LOFT* can fall under their society. God is using people I know and new acquaintances in so many unbelievable ways to make this happen. His mighty network is up and running!

Furthermore, He is raising up National Indian believers who share our same passion and want to serve alongside us, as well as couples here in the States who feel led to move to India to live full-time and serve with LOFT. In fact, just a few nights ago, a new couple in our church approached to tell me God was calling them to our mission too!

Following God's call with these strong desires in my heart, I humbly preside over *LOFT 218*. Please consider partnering with us prayerfully, financially, and personally by going with us to "Rise Up and Build" for the least of these as we make a difference for Christ!

The entire Parkison family

For more information about

Kelly McCorkle Parkison

and

He Knows Her Name
please visit:
www.facebook.com/kellymparkison
www.kellymccorkleparkison.com

To find out more about

Loft 218
please visit:
www.loft218.org

For more information about
AMBASSADOR INTERNATIONAL
please visit:

www.ambassador-international.com
@AmbassadorIntl
www.facebook.com/AmbassadorIntl